BARREL RACING

Ride Safe My Smart!
Your friend,
Sharon Camarillo

BARREL RACING

FOR FUN AND FAST TIMES

SHARON CAMARILLO

Skyhorse Publishing

Skyhorse Publishing books may be purchased in bulk at special discounts for sales promotion, corporate gifts, fund-raising, or educational purposes. Special editions can also be created to specifications. For details, contact the Special Sales Department, Skyhorse Publishing, 307 West 36th Street, 11th Floor, New York, NY 10018 or info@skyhorsepublishing.com.

www.skyhorsepublishing.com

10 9 8 7 6 5 4 3 2

Library of Congress Cataloging-in-Publication Data

Camarillo, Sharon.
Barrel racing for fun and fast times: winning tips for the horse and rider / Sharon Camarillo.
p. cm.
ISBN 978-1-60239-784-2
1. Barrel racing. I. Title.
GV1834.45.B35C38 2009
791.8'4–dc22
2009039630

Printed in China

I dedicate this book to . . .

Bob and Avril Meffan, my parents, and Wade, my son, who remain my biggest fans;

Donna Irvin, Cheryl Price, and Susan Van Rein, my coinstructors and fellow cowgirls, who share my passion for lifelong learning and equine education;

David Hayes, my friend and consulting veterinarian, who possesses the courage to defend the horse while developing our understanding of equine behavior;

Denise Calef, ProSportsPix, for her artistic design, technical advice, and guidance;

Debbie Wood, my friend and business associate, who shared her insight and guidance in the development of the Clinic and Classic programs;

The horses I have ridden, and my students and friends, who for the past thirty five years have allowed me to pursue my passion of building the horse–rider relationship through education and awareness.

Contents

Contents

Acknowledgments

I would like to thank Denise and Ron Calef for their tireless efforts to design and develop the artistic concept behind this book, including its chapter and cover artwork.

Cyndy Smith, for her photography and her contribution to the organization at Camp Camarillo.

Dorothy Peth, for her support and illustrations.

Erica Friedman; Tres Amigas, for her friendship and support of the Sharon Camarillo programs.

My Black Hawk College interns, Carly Hagey and Katie Chaffin, for their organization of tack and conditioning of horses. Many thanks and happy trails!

Cheryl Price, for her inspiration; wisdom and wit; technical advice; and editing skills. Her efforts ensured that this book became a reality. Cheryl, you are my champion and I thank you.

Catherine Frazier, the island in the sun who radiates brightness and lends her superior intellect and wholehearted support to every project that I dream up!

THANKS TO YOU ALL!

INTRODUCTION

Barrel Racing for Fun and Fast Times is a collection of motivational essays and tips designed to enlighten and inspire, not only barrel racers, but also all equine enthusiasts who wish to follow this path of success and personal satisfaction. As an accomplished horsewoman and National Finals Rodeo Qualifier many times over, Sharon is one of only a few women to be recognized by both the National Cowboy Hall of Fame and the National Cowgirl Museum and Hall of Fame for her advocacy of the equine and western lifestyle. Sharon has been a saddle and tack designer for over thirty years, and the Sharon Camarillo Collection logo has established itself as a highly coveted retail item.

A business graduate of California State Polytechnic University, Sharon believes in the power of education and encourages her students to enjoy the daily process that is necessary to develop trusting and rewarding relationships with their horses.

Sharon has established herself as a world-renowned equine clinician. Her program has been taught in forty states, Canada, Europe, Australia, and South America. Sharon is an American Quarter Horse Association Professional Horseman and has collaborated with her accomplished performance team to compile proven tips to help every horse owner achieve success in equine management, training, and rewarding competition. The team states: "Our collective goal is to share winning formulas that help inspire riders to establish working relationships with their equine partners and provide horsemanship techniques that contribute to safe, successful, and rewarding influences on the horses they ride in whatever disciplines they choose."

The following is a list of her traveling team of professional horsemen and educators that contribute to the success of her equine programs.

David Hayes, DVM, equine veterinarian, educator, certified journeyman farrier, equine chiropractor, and equine dentist, has been Sharon's consulting veterinarian for the last thirty-five years. He has been an invited speaker for both the American Association of Equine Practitioners and the American Farriers Association's Annual Conventions, where he presented his One-Step Horsemanship Program. An American Quarter Horse Association Breeder and Professional Horseman, Dr. Hayes's passion and understanding of equine physiology and behavior have helped thousands of rider and horse's lives.

Donna Irvin is a former Dodge National Circuit Rodeo finalist, equine professor, and equestrian coach for the nationally ranked Black Hawk College Equestrian Team in Kewanee, Illinois. Donna resides in Galva, Illinois, with her husband John, a performance horseshoer. Donna is a top professional barrel racer and an AQHA Professional Horseman. Donna travels with Sharon during academic breaks. Donna spent her professional sabbatical working on several projects, horse fairs, and professional rodeo competitions with Sharon in California.

Cheryl Machin-Price is the coauthor of *The A.R.T. of Barrel Racing*, a best-selling Western horseman book, and an AQHA Professional Horseman. Cheryl is a registered nurse by trade, and resides with her husband Jim in Washington State. Cheryl and Jim travel with Sharon to produce her Performance Horsemanship for Better Barrel Racing Clinics throughout the world. Cheryl's exceptional horsemanship skills and her ability to coach riders to their personal best come from her foundation in dressage and her early affiliation with the United States Pony Club.

Susan Van Rein is a professional horse trainer and competition barrel racer. She is an equine professor at Sierra College in Rocklin, California, and lives with her husband Jerry on a small ranch where they raise cattle and train horses. Susan's background is in English riding and dressage. Using her strong equestrian foundation, she later transferred her focus toward reining and roping events. Her passion today is horsemanship; her primarily discipline is barrel racing. Susan instructs at many of Sharon's performance horsemanship programs throughout the country.

FOREWORD

I had heard the name Sharon Camarillo and knew she was held in the highest esteem by the western community. When my company decided to create the National Barrel Horse Association, I was privileged to meet and get to know her. It was clear to me from the very beginning that her reputation was entirely justified and well deserved.

Sharon raises the bar for first class in everything that she touches. Her business savvy, the way she presents herself, and her talents in barrel racing and rodeo announcing are second to none.

She is always prepared. Sharon has the ability to connect with students at clinics. Her sweet, genuine nature makes students want to emulate her.

I am certain that this book will benefit all those who read it. I have personally benefited just by knowing her. It is an honor to be considered her friend.

Pete May
President, National Barrel
Horse Association

ONE

CONFORMATION CHARACTERISTICS FOR ATHLETIC PERFORMANCE

To achieve a high level of excellence, one must invest a high level of commitment.

Selecting the Right Horse for YOU

Your mind is made up. The search for the new horse begins. This huge decision comes with equal responsibility from both seller's and buyer's. It requires an honest representation of the horse's ability on the part of seller's and buyer's need to realistically identify their competitive goals and the limit of their financial resources. If the horse and the prospective buyer's level of expertise do not match, a responsible seller prohibits the sale. The horse is then prevented from being purchased by someone who would prevent him from performing at his level of training, producing a frustrating environment for both the horse and the new buyer.

It's not a perfect world, and sales that create inappropriate combinations of rider and horse occur every day. If the buyer or seller is inexperienced in the sales process, consideration should be given to obtaining the services of an agent. There are many benefits of having a reputable agent. First, the professional agent is trained to assess the skill level of the horse and the rider. Although the agent obtains a commission from the sale of the horse, the reputation they obtain from finding the right horse for the right person is what provides longevity in their profession. When you interview potential agents ask for references from sellers and buyers they have represented. Identify in a written document the fee for service and the agreed-upon services to be provided by the agent. This "contract" includes disclosure statements from the seller regarding competitive records, health issues, and the individual horse's vices. It is in the best interest of the horse, the seller, and the buyer for the seller to communicate all pertinent information to the potential buyer.

If the potential *seller* chooses to make the decision on his own without the service of an agent, the following tips may be helpful.

Tips for the Seller:

◈ Allow the buyer to observe the entire process of retrieving the horse from the pasture or stall. Ask him to watch the grooming and saddling process. Discuss any "quirks" that the horse may have.

◈ Review any individual shoeing issues during the grooming process.

◈ Tell the buyer if the horse needs to be lunged before riding.

◈ Ride the horse first. This allows the buyer to see what the horse is capable of doing.

◈ It is now time for the buyer to ride the horse. It is in the best interest of all for you to remain in the arena while the buyer rides the horse in case the level of expertise of the potential buyer was not correctly identified. The most solid "bomb-proof" horse can become a danger if the rider does not have the required skills. Intervene and ask the buyer to step down if there is potential for injury.

◈ Ask the buyer get used to the controllability of the horse by completing circles, directional changes, stops, leads, and lateral work; again this depends on the horse's level of training and the rider's ability.

◈ If you are satisfied that the skill level of both the horse and buyer is acceptable, it is time take the horse to the barrel pattern. Invite the buyer to ride the horse through the pattern once or twice at the speed both horse and rider are comfortable.

◈ If you believe there is a potential match it is time for the second phase of the evaluation. Here you have two options. Your first option is to take the horse to a competition or simulated competition and allow the buyer to "make a run." Identify the size of the pattern, preferably a standard size course, with an electric timer available. The second option is to ask the buyer to attend a competition where the horse is currently competing.

If the potential *buyer* chooses to make the decision on his own without the service of an agent, the following tips may be helpful.

Tips for the Buyer:

◈ Observe the horse as the seller retrieves, grooms, saddles, and rides.

◈ Learn from the seller what riding methods were used in training the horse. Identify if the horse's foundation of training and ability is correct and honestly represented.

◈ When you feel comfortable enough to ride the horse through the barrel course, evaluate the elements of the pattern in terms of the approach, rate, and turn, and determine if the horse's strengths and weaknesses are acceptable to you.

◈ If you have a high interest in the horse, ask to take the horse to a competition or to attend a competition where the horse is scheduled to compete.

◈ If the seller declines any reasonable request consider this to be a red flag.

◈ Ask specific questions but do not be argumentative.
  ♦ Does the horse bleed?
  ♦ Is the horse prone to tying up?
  ♦ Has the horse ever had colic?
  ♦ Have there been any major surgeries or illnesses? Has the horse been X–rayed? Are medical records available?
  ♦ Does the horse have any respiratory problems or require any special medications?
  ♦ Does the horse haul?
  ♦ What is the seller's routine care in terms of nutrition and training?

Honestly assess if you have the resources to address any of the weaknesses the horse has.

Once you have completed the initial evaluation of the horse's performance and discussed any medical or performance deficits, make a decision if the horse is a serious prospect for you.

The final, informed, and educated decision should be placed in the hands of a professional. The buyer should contact his personal veterinarian, if available, or a recommended veterinarian in the area for a pre-purchase consultation and soundness examination. The more information obtained the better the decision the buyer will be able to make.

The bottom line is that full disclosure on both the seller's and the prospective buyer's part results in the best outcome for everyone involved. As caregivers of horses, we are expected to provide the very best for them. We need to consider all aspects of horsemanship. It is difficult to overcome a deficiency in one area by over-achieving in another. Good horses deserve good lives, and there is nothing more rewarding than to have a strong relationship with your horse. Remember, you are investing not only time but financial resources for the horse's health and well-being. Good luck and good purchasing!

TIP 1   Selecting Athletic Conformation

While there seem to be horses of many different conformational shapes and sizes competing successfully in barrel racing, it is important to remember to look for appropriate conformation for the chosen discipline when you are selecting a potential prospect. It is unfair and unproductive to expect a horse to make the types of maneuvers, especially at speed, that are required of the barrel horse if the horse is unbalanced to handle the job. Some rules of thumb are: the hind end should appear larger than the front end, the top line should be shorter than the underline, the cannon bones should be shorter than the forearm/gaskin, and the stifle should be wider than the hip.

TIP 2   The Importance of a Veterinary Pre-Purchase Exam

You may choose to seek the opinion of a professional veterinary examiner who is not personally involved in the sale. However, as the buyer, it is always best to use your own veterinarian, if possible; your own veterinarian will be familiar with the physical

demands placed on a barrel horse and with your abilities as a rider. The consulting veterinarian should review prior medical and surgical records and evaluate the physical and mental condition of the horse. Expect stress and flexion tests to be done to assess the horse's current condition. Radiographs may be necessary for an "in-depth" view. One of the most important functions of a pre-purchase exam is that it slows down the sale. This delay allows for better, and usually more rational, decisions.

TIP 3 Important Questions to Ask During a Pre-Purchase Exam

These questions may seem simplistic but they provide valuable information.

❖ What is the age of the horse?
❖ What has the horse been used for in the past?

◈ Who has owned the horse in the past? (Not just the current owner.)

◈ Who trained the horse?

◈ Does the horse have any present or previous lameness issues?

◈ Has the horse had any surgeries? Colic?

◈ What has been the extent of veterinary care the horse has received?

◈ When was the horse last vaccinated and de-wormed?

◈ What type of dental problems has the horse had and what dental treatment has the horse received?

◈ Is the horse difficult to shoe?

◈ Does the horse have any vices such as cribbing, stall weaving, pulling back, trailer issues, or any other issues that a buyer should know about?

Buying a horse can be a fun experience, but it takes a lot of work, time, and experience to find the right one. Buying a barrel horse is an even more difficult job because we are all looking for the special athlete that is able and willing to win. A horse with a former winning season is like a stock in the stock market . . . a glorious history does not ensure future success.

TWO

CARE AND CONDITIONING OF THE BARREL HORSE

To study horsemanship, one needs an attitude of compassion, awareness, patience, forgiveness, and confidence.

A Special Thank You to Our Equine Partners

To have a horse in your life is a gift. In the matter of a few short years, a horse can teach a young girl courage, if she chooses to grab mane and hang on for dear life. Even the smallest of ponies is mightier than the tallest of girls. To conquer the fear of falling off, having one's toes crushed, or being publicly humiliated at a horse show is an admirable feat for any child. For that, we can be grateful.

Horses teach us responsibility. Unlike a bicycle or a computer, a horse needs regular care and most of it requires that you get dirty and smelly and up off the couch. Choosing to leave your cozy kitchen to break the crust of ice off the water buckets is to choose responsibility. When our horses dip their noses and drink heartily, we know we've made the right choice.

Learning to care for a horse is both an art and a science. Some are easy keepers, requiring little more than regular turnout, a flake of hay, and a trough of clean water. Others will test you—you'll struggle to keep them from being too fat or too thin. You'll have their feet shod regularly only to find shoes gone missing. Some are so accident-prone you'll swear they're intentionally finding new ways to injure themselves.

If you weren't raised with horses, you can't know that they have unique personalities. You'd expect this from dogs, but horses? Indeed, there are clever horses, grumpy horses, and even horses with a sense of humor. Those prone to humor will test you by finding new ways to escape from the barn when you least expect it.

Horses can be timid or brave, athletic or lazy, obstinate or willing. You will hit it off with some horses and others will elude you altogether. There are as many "types" of horses as there are people, which makes the whole partnership thing all the more interesting.

If you've never ridden a horse, you probably assume it's a simple thing you can learn in a weekend. You can, in fact, learn the basics on a Sunday, but to truly ride well takes a lifetime. Working with a living being is far more complex than turning a key in the ignition and putting the car or tractor in "drive."

In addition to listening to your instructor, your horse will have a few things to say to you as well. On a good day, he'll be happy to go along with the program and tolerate your mistakes; on a bad day, you'll swear he's trying to kill you. Perhaps he's naughty or perhaps he's fed up with how slowly you're learning his language. Regardless, the horse will have an opinion. He may choose to challenge you (which can ultimately make you a better rider) or he may carefully carry you over fences—if it suits him. It all depends on the partnership—and partnership is what it's all about.

If you face your fears, swallow your pride, and are willing to work at it, you'll learn lessons in courage, commitment, and compassion in addition to basic survival skills. You'll discover just how hard you're willing to work toward a goal, how little you know, and how much you have to learn.

And, while some people think the horse "does all the work," you'll be challenged physically as well as mentally. Your horse may humble you completely. Or, you may find that sitting on his back is the closest you'll get to heaven.

You can choose to intimidate your horse, but do you really want to? The results may come more quickly, but will your work ever be as graceful as that gained through trust? The best partners choose to listen, as well as to tell. When it works, we experience a sweet sense of accomplishment brought about by smarts, hard work, and mutual understanding between horse and rider. These are the days when you know with absolute certainty that your horse is enjoying his work.

If we make it to adulthood with horses still in our lives, most of us have to squeeze riding into our oversaturated schedules, balancing our need for things equine with those of our households and employers. There is never enough time to ride, or to ride as well as we'd like. Hours in the barn are stolen pleasures.

If it is in your blood to love horses, you share your life with them. Our horses know our secrets; we braid our tears into their manes and whisper our hopes into their ears. A barn is a sanctuary in an unsettled world, a sheltered place where life's true priorities are clear: a warm place to sleep, someone who loves us, and the luxury of regular meals. Some of us need these reminders.

When you step back, it's not just about horses—it's about love, life, and learning. On any given day, a friend is celebrating the birth of a foal, a blue ribbon, or recovery from an illness. That same day, there is also loss: a broken limb, a case of colic, a decision to sustain a life or end it gently. As horse people, we share the accelerated life cycle of horses: the hurried rush of life, love, loss, and death that caring for these animals brings us. When our partners pass, it is more than a moment of sorrow.

We mark our loss with words of gratitude for the ways our lives have been blessed. Our memories are of joy, awe, and wonder. Absolute union. We honor our horses for their brave hearts, courage, and willingness to give.

—Author unknown

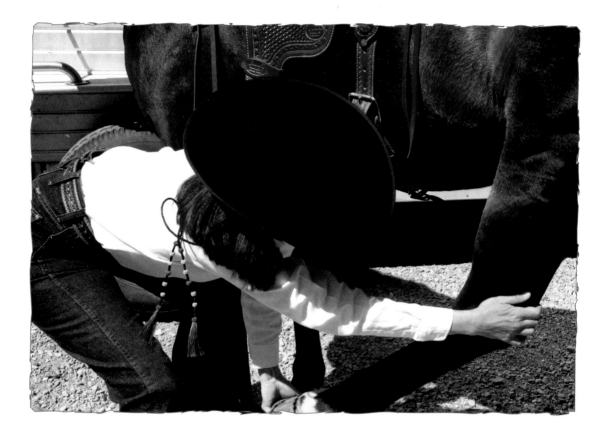

TIP 1 Daily and Pre-Competition Stretches

All athletes take time to warm up and stretch out their muscles before the actual workout or competition. Our equine athletes require the same preparation. Remember to warm the muscles up before you stretch them, and don't force a stretch. By incorporating the stretches in your daily work, your horse accepts the stretches more readily, and you increase your horse's range of motion. It also helps detect any soreness or tightness your horse may be experiencing.

TIP 2 Nutrition and Conditioning for Your Equine Athlete

It takes more than just pulling your horse out of the pasture and loading him in the trailer for you to do well at a competition. A healthy diet and exercise program is essential, so if you are ready for competition make sure your preparation devotes attention to conditioning and nutrition. Successful outcomes and injury-free runs are the result of healthy, conditioned, and properly nourished equine athletes.

As a rule of thumb, a mature horse should consume one and one-half to two pounds of good quality hay for every 100 pounds of its weight on a daily basis. Hay is the foundation of a balanced diet. Grass hay or a mix of grass-alfalfa is what I prefer to feed, with protein levels never rising above 18 percent, and much lower depending on the activity level of the horse. Protein levels of grass hay run from 8 percent to 10 percent and remain a good feed source for horses that display naturally high amounts of energy. Because horses are foraging animals, 70 percent of their diet should be made up of hay or pasture. I always choose hay over pellet feeds. Loose hay reduces the propensity for colic, choking, and gives a nervous horse something to do.

You should only add concentrated grain mixtures, vitamins, and mineral supplements as required by the individual horse and his nutritional needs. Too much grain can produce additional energy that can translate into behavioral problems. I keep the protein level below 12 percent and choose an oat base feed for the digestive well-being of the athlete. I feed minimal amounts of grain depending on the activity level of the horse I am feeding. I also choose to add fat to my horse's daily diet for increased calories

on a hard keeper and for coat condition and well-being. Rice bran is the fat choice that works for me.

Some competitors choose to add two tablespoons of loose table salt to their horse's daily diet, along with a free choice trace-mineral salt block to aid in hydration. While traveling, increase the salt intake to four tablespoons daily.

TIP 3 Conditioning the Performance Horse

Depending on the discipline, it takes a minimum of five miles of aerobic conditioning at least three days per week to produce visible results. Enhancing physical condition reduces the risk of muscle fatigue and strain, which could result in injury during training and competition, brought on by overwork and poor ground conditions.

TIP 4 Sprinting the Performance Horse

Barrel racing is an actual race against the clock, a one-horse race! I like to simulate a "work," as trainers call it on the race track, once per month. Haul if necessary to a facility or location where you have access to a track, good ground, etc. On the day of the "work," plan for a precise and effective exercise. Choose a snaffle-type training bridle. Walk one-quarter mile, trot one-quarter mile, and lope one-quarter mile for warm-up before extending to a full-out gallop. When you think you have all the speed that your horse has to give, pick up your over-under and ask one time for any extra

speed that the horse has in reserve. One hundred and fifty to two hundred yards is enough distance at full speed. Ease down slowly and gradually bring your horse back to the trot. It is critical to take appropriate time to thoroughly cool the horse down and allow his breathing to return to normal. The cooldown could take up to two miles of slow walking and trotting.

This "work" constitutes a day's exercise reduced to about a thirty-minute ride. Follow the cooldown with a bath, a rub down with liniment, and some turn out. This "work" gets a horse wanting to reach and run.

Rarely do our horses get to run full out, even during competition. Your horse may be a little stiff the day following this "work." Especially if you don't follow with a good cool down.horse is a little stiff the following day, especially if you do not follow up the work with a good cool down.

TIP 5 Cooling Out the Performance Horse

Always remember to finish any conditioning exercise, training session, or competition with a complete and thorough cool out. This should take one to two miles and should take up to twenty minutes, allowing the horse to regain regularity in his breathing. Incorporate walking and, at minimum, a trot or jog into the cool-down process. The horse can have as much water as he wants to drink at this time.

When the ride is over, find a place to make a crisp finish, get off, un-cinch, and reward the horse's effort. The horse needs to know when he is on task and when his job is complete. Un-cinching is usually a signal to the horse that the ride is over.

Follow with a liniment rub down, bath or body wash, and a possible turn out.

TIP 6 Knowing Your Horse's Normals

Know what is normal for your horse. Being able to take your horse's heart rate, respiratory rate, and temperature are important skills to have. A normal equine heart rate is usually between thirty-six to forty beats per minute, resting respiratory rate is eight to twelve per minute, and normal temperature is 99°F to 101.5°F. To completely cool out your horse after a workout or competition continue the cooldown until the heart rate and respiratory rate return to your horse's normal levels. Your veterinarian can help you in this learning process. Immediately notify your veterinarian if abnormal temperature or symptoms arise.

TIP 7 Supplying Adequate Fresh Water

Remember, a horse can drink up to ten gallons of water during stall rest at night, especially in the summer. Make sure when on the road that you haul enough buckets to accommodate your horse's needs. Allowing the horse to drink his fill of water before bedding him down for the night and leaving full buckets of water in the stall should be sufficient. If buckets are empty by morning, additional water should be provided. If the strange taste of a new water sources causes your horse to turn up his nose and avoid drinking, adding a can of Coke or a package of Kool-Aid to camouflage the taste can help with the transition.

TIP 8 General Tips for Locating Lameness

Lameness in a limb is usually indicated by the horse minimizing the use of the limb by:

◆ Spending the least amount of time with that foot on the ground
◆ Shortening the stride of that limb
◆ Changing the arc of the stride
◆ Not landing with that hoof level with the ground
◆ Standing with that leg placed "out of normal position"
◆ Shifting weight off the affected leg, either flexing at the knee or "cocking a hip"
◆ Standing with a raised heel or toe
◆ Having a painful response to hoof testers
◆ Showing a painful response to flexing or extension of a particular joint
◆ Mild shivering or shaking of the leg after exercise
◆ Pounding digital pulse felt at the fetlock

When trotting on firm, level ground a horse usually nods or raise its head when the sore front leg is about to contact the ground, and drops its head when a lame hind leg is about to hit the ground. It is necessary to know the normal level of the head when the horse is not lame to establish what is abnormal.

TIP 9 Good Dentistry and Good Teeth

Research has shown that the teeth, jaw, and head provide valuable information to the brain that affects the horse's total movement. Teeth and the hyoid bone, located between the jaws, act like a gyroscope for the horse, determining body position in relationship to the ground. Aside from eating, good teeth and dentistry are critical for the well-being of the horse. Teeth affect the movement of the jaw, and the jaw affects the entire balance and "handle ability" of the horse. Any form of snaffle bit pulls the horse's lips back against the front cheek teeth, potentially causing pain and alteration in head carriage. This directly influences acceptance of a bit, and impedes athletic performance. Teeth are constantly changing shape. To maintain a healthy and sound horse, a competent veterinary dentist should perform a dental examination annually.

TIP 10 — The Functional Hoof and Proper Shoeing

We all know the adage "no hoof, no horse." No truer words could be spoken. Yet, too often, we forget this wisdom. Bad feet may work for a while but will ultimately adversely affect the horse's performance.

Assuming the horse's legs are straight and correct, check to make sure that:

◆ The hooves are positioned directly beneath the bony column.
◆ The hooves are symmetrical when viewed from the front, with no flared walls.
◆ There is alignment of the hoof and pastern axis when viewed from the side.
◆ The slope of the toe and the heel are the same.
◆ The hoof is of adequate size to support the horse.
◆ The shoe shape matches the properly trimmed hoof.
◆ The shoe provides sufficient lateral and posterior support to the hoof.

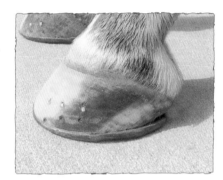

TIP 11 — Horseshoeing Tips

Taking your horse to a good farrier every six weeks is a must. Three things to look for in good shoeing include: 1) hooves that are trimmed so that they're level and balanced; 2) shoes that fit full as they run past the heels and line up slightly to the outside of the walls; and 3) clinches that are smooth—run your hand over the outside hoof wall to check.

Rim shoes are a good choice. They are lightweight and provide good traction on most types of ground. Consider pads on the front feet if you ride on gravel or on rocky or hard ground. Pads are inexpen-

sive insurance against bruises and they do not interfere with traction. When traveling always carry an extra set of shoes shaped for your horse in case you lose a shoe at a competition.

TIP 12 **Equine Rest and Relaxation**

Afternoon baths and turn out is a great way to relax and refresh horses' minds and bodies. While on the road, I even look for a stream I can lead or ride my horses into if I cannot find a pasture for relaxation. It feels great to let cold water run up to the knees or even deeper if safe conditions apply.

TIP 13 Maintaining Soundness and Well-Being of the Performance Horse

Barrel horses are fine-tuned, high performance athletes, much like high speed race-cars. Top performing barrel horses require the best of care and maintenance. Like a racecar, barrel horses have big motors that generate incredible force. This puts strain on their bodies and stress on their frame, causing sore joints, strained tendons, pulled muscles, and skeletal misalignment. Proper care and maintenance of your horse helps

you stay competitive and reduces the chance of a career-threatening injury. Regular management of your horse must include: timely and correct hoof care, including trimming and shoeing; good body conditioning and effective nutrition personalized for the needs of the athlete; attention and maintenance of equipment; and proper veterinary care, consistent and effective vaccination and deworming schedules, annual dental exams, and veterinary chiropractic and neuromuscular adjustments as needed.

TIP 14 Keeping Your Horse Healthy While on the Road

Problems to avoid:

◈ Stress from hauling that can lead to ulcers
◈ Dehydration
◈ Respiratory problems from poor air quality
◈ Hauling fatigue

Depending on the nature of the horse, discuss with your equine veterinarian whether or not preloading with some type of ulcer-prevention medication would be a wise choice for the well-being of the horse. Research on the stress of hauling as a cause of ulcers was not previously available, but current research shows that even short hauls can prove very stressful for the horse.

To help keep the horse hydrated, add two tablespoons of salt to his daily diet, increasing to two tablespoons twice per day a few days before the horse is to be hauled. There is a great amount of information available that explains the importance of adding salt to the horse's diet to avoid dehydration and replace the salts (sodium) lost during strenuous exercise. Once dehydration is noticed, electrolytes, including salt, should not be used without the supervision of a veterinarian.

Antioxidants are a great resource to reinforce the horse's immune system while traveling to new environments, often under stressful conditions.

Feeding free-choice trace minerals, good quality hay, and concentrates only to the extent the horse needs it are important for the health of the horse; research shows that the horse can only digest two pounds of concentrate at a time. Fresh water is essential for a horse, and changing to different water supplies presents its own set of problems. Try flavoring the water to help camouflage strange tastes. If practical,

take your feed and hay from home in order to keep the horse's diet as consistent as possible.

Work with your veterinarian to help formulate a plan that works for your individual horse. It's a good idea to ask your veterinarian if you may phone him from the road with additional questions or concerns.

TIP 15 Creating a Winning Environment

All horses deserve attention, especially horses used for competition. Consistent schedules are imperative. These revolve around feeding, exercise, training, and tune-ups. I usually plan the Monday after a weekend competition as a day off. Pasture turn out, or just being allowed to move about in an outdoor pen, is a nice way to mentally relax and work the horse's tight muscles. Tuesday through Thursday I combine conditioning routines necessary for physical strength and stamina with gymnastic exercises designed to enhance performance. I plan at least one fast run in the training pen before a weekend of competition. This helps put competition on my mind and helps maximize both horse and rider performance when the pressure is on in competition.

Try experimenting with this formula: Take one mile at a walk to loosen and relax muscles and one mile at an extended trot to tighten abdominal muscles and work on length of stride. Then take one to two miles at a gallop, depending on the horse. The gallop is great aerobic conditioning, a way to increase lung capacity, strength, and muscle tone. The gallop is faster than the lope. You need to maintain an extension in stride for the biggest benefit.

The conditioning exercises should be done outside the arena if the resource is available. If your arena is the only or the safest area to ride, use the walk to loosen and relax muscles. Long trot down the long side of the arena, collect the stride, and maintain a collected trot or jog on the shorter side of the arena, before extending the stride back down the long side of the arena. Calculate at least a mile at the trot. Add a lope or gallop for approximately five to seven minutes in order to build and maintain lung capacity for maximum performance in most timed events. A sprint down the long side of the arena or along the side of a country road increases a horse's incentive to reach and run.

I have had great luck swimming horses. Consult your professional for specific details, but as I remember, I used the pool three times per week beginning with three minutes and building up to seven minutes. This is a great option to freshen horses that have been on the road and are feeling a little flat or tired, especially when trying to gain the edge for an important competition like the National Finals Rodeo. Swimming is also a great resource for older horses that have physical challenges that prohibit them from doing the roadwork necessary to maintain competitive condition. Remember, though, that there is some roadwork involved in any swimming therapy. Again, I challenge the reader to be creative and research options.

TIP 16 Have Faith in Your Equine Professionals

Your equine professionals, including your choice of veterinarian, dentist, horseshoer, and body worker are truly your "pit crew." Each of these trained professionals has a vested interest in your success because they are part of it. If you don't feel you are getting the attention or advice you need, it may be time to research a replacement. However, keep in mind that there may be some advice you are not ready or willing to take, especially if it interferes with your competition schedule. If you have confidence in your "pit crew," heed their advice and recommendations. Timely and proper veterinary support is critical to your horse's health and well-being.

Unfortunately, horse owners often shoot themselves in the foot when trying to minimize their financial burden in regard to veterinary and professional care. Riders are quick to look for alternative sources for success: miracle cures, magic feeds, or new saddles or bridles promising faster runs and more control. They lose sight of commonsense good husbandry practices which include regular veterinary assistance from competent veterinarians who are well versed in their event of choice. Choose your pit crew wisely; your career depends on them!

TIP 17 Warning!

My consulting veterinarian, Dr. David Hayes, stands on the fact that the popularly used pain reliever Banamine should *never* be administered into the muscle, regardless of what the label says. Dr. Dave has kept my horses sound and in competitive condition for over thirty years, and, with that said, I stand with Dr. Dave and strongly recommend against medically treating one's horse because it isn't acting right, or hazardously giving the drug just because "it won't hurt the horse, right?" It is important to use one's common sense and protect a valuable investment by having the horse diagnosed and treated by a competent veterinarian. Unfortunately, barrel racers are notorious for doing their own veterinary work, frequently at the expense of their horse. For the welfare of the horse I encourage veterinary involvement before administering any medication. Nobody ever promised that owning a horse was risk-free or inexpensive.

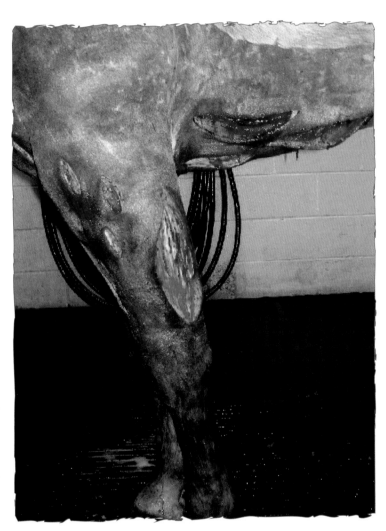

THREE

TRAINING, TUNE-UP, AND COMPETITION EQUIPMENT

Quality equipment influences training outcomes.

In my life, horses were answers to my prayers. Dreaming of owning my own horse carried me through my teenage years, and horse competition provided me an opportunity for a university education. My association with the horses that have come in and out of my life, whether owned or not, elevated me to national recognition and has been the foundation for my recreation and occupation.

I am a cowgirl and proud to be one. I found this essay profound and appropriate and wish to dedicate it to the horses we own; the horses we have known, regardless of breed or discipline; and to my readers, horse owners or not, who truly love and admire horses.

"Just a Horse"

From time to time, people tell me, "Lighten up, it's just a horse," or, "That's a lot of money for just a horse." They don't understand the distance traveled, the time spent, or the costs involved for "just a horse." Some of my proudest moments have come about with "just a horse." Many hours have passed and my only company was "just a horse," but I did not once feel slighted. Some of my saddest moments have been brought about by "just a horse," and in those days of darkness, the gentle touch of "just a horse" gave me comfort and reason to overcome the dark. Those who think it's "just a horse" probably also use phrases like "just a friend," "just a sunrise," or "just a promise." "Just a horse" brings into my life the very essence of friendship, trust, and pure unbridled joy. "Just a horse" brings out the compassion and patience that makes me a better person. Because of "just a horse" I rise early, take long walks, and look longingly to the future.

So for folks like me, it's not "just a horse" but an embodiment of all the hopes and dreams of the future, the fond memories of the past, and the pure joy of the moment. "Just a horse" brings out what's good in me and diverts my thoughts away from myself and the worries of the day. I hope that someday others have the opportunity to understand that it's not "just a horse" but the thing that gives me humanity and keeps me from being "just a woman." So the next time you hear the phrase "just a horse," smile. You are one of the blessed few that understand.

—Author unknown

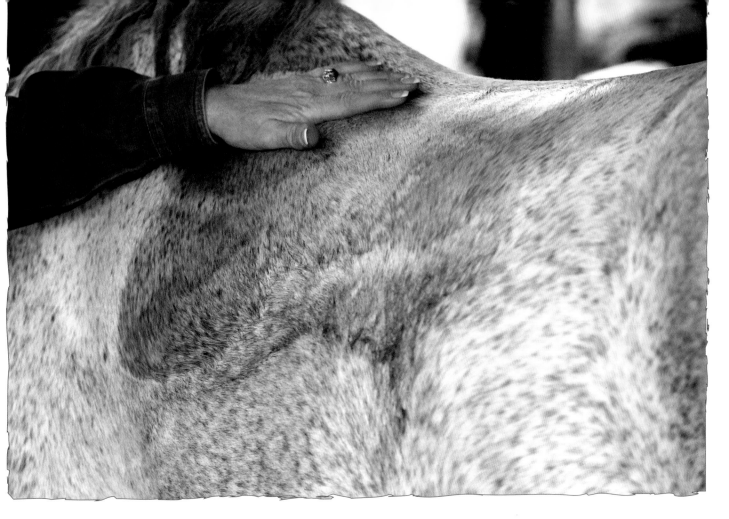

TIP 1   Fitting the Saddle to the Horse

When our boots don't fit, we are aware that it not only affects our sore and blistered feet but also produces back and leg pain, not to mention what the pain or discomfort does to our attitude. Horses don't have the luxury of verbalizing discomfort, but they do communicate to their intuitive rider through irregular movement and poor performance. Improper saddle fit also results in poor attitude and lameness. Pay attention to sweat patterns after each ride. An even sweat pattern usually reflects an appropriate saddle fit. Haul your horse to a professional saddle maker or responsible retailer for saddle fitting questions.

TIP 2   Fitting the Saddle to the Rider

Not only is it mandatory that the saddle tree mirrors the shape of the horse's back for proper fit, but the size of the seat needs to complement the rider's body type and choice of disciplines as well. The correct seat size varies greatly with the equine disci-

pline. For example, I weigh 130 pounds and stand 5 feet 6 inches. I choose a 14-inch seat for barrel racing but would use a larger seat, for example, in the sport of cutting. Regardless of the discipline, a saddle seat that is too small for a rider allows the rider to tilt forward and lose his seat in performance. The ability to maintain a flexible pelvis rotation is critical in using your seat to communicate to the horse. I suggest at least a two-finger measurement between the rider's thigh and the saddle swell. This is critical to the rider's ability to maintain mobility and flexibility.

TIP 3 Saddle Pads

The choice of saddle pad will depend on the horse's saddle and how well it fits the horse. Ideally, the bars of the saddle mirror the horses back. A three-quarter inch pad adds an extra cushion for the well-fitted saddle. Many of the horses today have "wither pockets" on their backs, which are the hollow areas behind the horse's shoulders on each side of the wither. This often creates an asymmetrical back that is tough to fit with any saddle. A Sure Fit pad by Reinsman Equestrian Products or a saddle pad with an adjustable build-up will be necessary to fill in this area.

There are several materials used in making saddle pads, and each has its own advantages. For example, felt absorbs moisture, while closed-cell foam pads help stabilize a saddle that rolls from side to side on a round-backed horse. Experiment with saddle

pads to make the best choice for your horse. I prefer natural materials that are designed to absorb moisture and cushion the saddle.

Elevate the front of your pad so that is rests against the gullet of the saddle, a short distance off the horse's withers, before you cinch your saddle. This helps minimize the possibility of the pad pinching or rubbing the withers.

TIP 4 Stirrup Options for Training and Competition

I believe that the crooked-style stirrup, with a wide, bell-bottomed base, makes a wonderful addition to any saddle. My preference is the three-inch base. Not only does the design offer stability for the lower leg, which directly influences upper body position, but it also decreases the discomfort in the rider's hips and knees that can result from long hours in the saddle. I believe that the design, combined with the wider base, stabilizes the rider and prevents torque of the lower leg and knee.

Another cause of rider instability is stiffness in the hips and lower back brought on by both tightness in the pelvis and gripping with the knees. Try to focus on keeping your joints relaxed. Practice riding with your foot parallel to your horse's side as opposed to the heel in toe out that is so common. This position will also allow the rider's calf to cue the horse for lateral and forward movement, a cueing technique helped by the design of the crooked stirrup.

When riding with a wide-based stirrup, remember, as a point of safety, to pull your boot almost completely out of the stirrup before stepping down off the horse. I also advise not using thick- or crepe-soled boots when riding in these stirrups, or any stirrup for that matter.

A balanced rider contributes to a balanced horse, and anything that improves the rider's position contributes to achieving that goal.

TIP 5 Training Bits

Bit selection is an important part of successful training and competition. Training bits, including the O-Ring, D-Ring, or Sweet Six Snaffles, offer direct control without the influence of leverage shanks. They are designed to help the rider isolate the five important parts of the horse's body identified in Chapter 6, Tip 1, in order to better communicate your instructions to your horse. Training equipment should be used to reinforce the horse's foundation, rebalance the horse, and correct problems that occur during competition. The bit of choice should provide direct control, without the influ-

ence of a shank, in order to reinforce rhythm, suppleness, and contact. Proper training equipment will also help teach and reinforce upward and downward gait transitions.

TIP 6   Introducing the Horse to the Leverage Bit

Transitioning to the leverage bit is an important part of the horse's training. This process can take up to several months, even years. Patience and understanding are critical to a successful transition from the direct control of the snaffle to the leverage of the competition bridle.

The simplest transition for the barrel racer is to select a balanced two- to four-inch shank, gag type, snaffle bit. In general, horses don't resist the bit, per se, as much as they react to the new pressure point added by the curb strap. Use the basic principle of applying pressure and then releasing to encourage your horse as he moves forward into the bridle. During this transition process have your equine dentist check your horse's mouth for soundness and appropriate development. Discuss the application of the bit seat with your dentist at this time.

The round pen is a safe place to begin this transition because it lets the horse move without the rider's influence on his back and allows him to get familiar with the new equipment. When neccessary, reinforce the horse's existing foundation by returning to the snaffle for review. Consider this transition as the step into equine junior high school, with graduation from high school and college as the ultimate goal. Some horses are brighter and more athletic students, and will adapt more quickly. *Patience and understanding of the process are keys to success, whatever the lesson.*

TIP 7 Selecting the Best Bit for Competition

Bits are as severe as the rider's hands that use them. A bigger bit does not necessarily translate into more control, and even the mildest design can become a lethal weapon in untrained hands. The journey from the training snaffle to a leverage bit takes time, patience, and understanding. Realize that when using the training snaffle, one pound of pressure from the rider's hand transfers one pound of pressure to the bit. When a bit with a shank is added, the pressure is magnified in proportion to the length of shank.

Again, use the round pen when changing equipment. This gives the horse a chance to experiment with the feel of different equipment. More aggressive bits should only be introduced when the horse understands what the rider is asking him to do and is confident enough to carry the bit without being intimidated or confused as pressure is introduced and increased. Once this stage of training is reached, it is time to begin the transition toward the bit that will control the horse as he progresses in his training.

When introducing new equipment, remember to continue the education of upward and downward gait transitions. Pay attention to maintaining softness throughout your horse's body. Use lateral rein and/or leg contact to help maintain control, rhythm, and softness, these being important elements of a well-bridled horse.

TIP 8 Finishing Your Horse "In the Bridle"

Ultimately, a trained horse should accept whatever bridle the educated rider chooses to use. Bits are a means of communication with the horse. The rider uses the reins to make the connection between the rider's hands and the horse's mouth, resulting in the appropriate body alignment, position, and gait transition. A trained rider and horse have a broad choice of bridle options. The horse is analogous to a student in high school, who needs a teacher (or in this case, a rider) who understands what is needed to complete the horse's education. In choosing competition equipment, the bottom line is how well it controls your horse in competition as speed is added.

TIP 9 Martingales versus Tie Downs

German martingales, typically, are used with direct control bits such as the O-Ring, D-Ring, or Sweet Six Snaffle bit. The German martingale can also be a training aid to help a horse make the transition to a leverage bit. I encourage the addition of a tie down for competition. Make sure, as with the introduction of any new equipment, that you put the tie

down on your horse and move the horse around in a round pen or on a lunge line before climbing on. This allows the horse to feel the new pressure points without the influence of the rider on his back. Be sure to move the horse from a walk to a trot, and from the trot to the lope, as the transition between gaits requires rebalance and is usually the moment when the horse notices the increased pressure of any new equipment. Begin with a neutral adjustment; the tie down strap should be able to touch the horse's throatlatch as the slack from the strap is removed.

There are several varieties of tie downs and straps. My preference is the leather noseband complemented with a leather tie down strap. A nylon strap and a rope noseband are more aggressive and provide additional control, if necessary. The guideline

I follow is that the martingales are used in training and transition while tie down options are introduced to the horse during the transition period in preparation for use in competition.

TIP 10 Using a Mechanical Hackamore as a Bridle Option

A mechanical hackamore refers to a bit-less bridle that is not a traditional braided rawhide or leather hackamore. A mechanical hackamore has steel shanks, a noseband, and some type of adjustable curb strap. It is designed to apply pressure across the bridge of the horse's nose and under the jaw. It produces the front to back control necessary for stopping or rating. Depending on the design, most mechanical hackamores offer very little lateral control, suppleness, or shoulder elevation, and should be combined in training with a snaffle bit in order to reinforce control in these areas. Make sure the noseband is balanced across the bridge of the horse's nose, and adjust the curb strap or

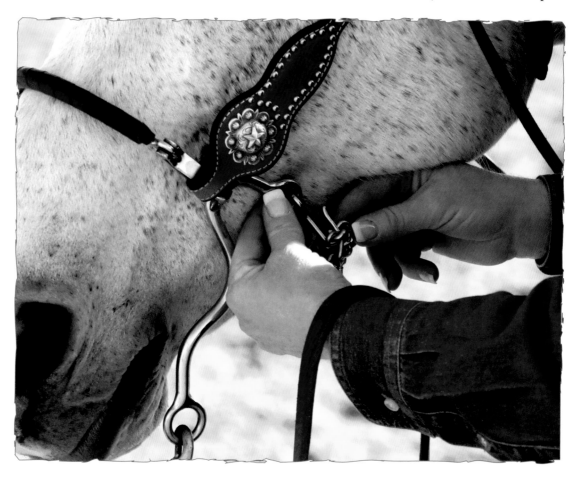

chain according to how much contact is necessary to achieve the desired results. The combination of hackamore and bit and the quick-stop hackamore are variations of the mechanical hackamore.

TIP 11 Adjusting Bits and Bridles

Adjusting any bridle takes some thought and an understanding of how the equipment has been designed to connect to pressure points on the horse's mouth, jaw, and head. The more gag the bit is designed to have, the more wrinkle and less curb pressure I adjust for. I adjust each bit according to its form and function. A gag bit is designed for suppleness and lateral control while the more solid bit usually offers more front to hind control. A good, neutral adjustment for any bit is to place the mouthpiece so that it meets the corners of the horse's mouth and allow for a two-finger

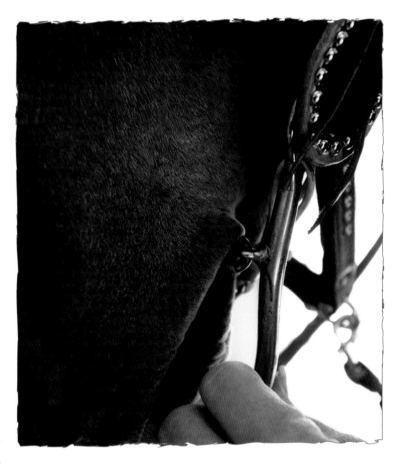

gap between the jaw and the curb strap. The bit and curb can be tightened or loosened from this neutral position according to the amount of contact and control required.

TIP 12 Tie Downs

In today's world of barrel racing competition, more riders choose not to use a tie down than do. Can I run my horses without a tie down? Yes. Do I choose to on a consistent basis? No. In the world of timed event competitions, we run in a variety of arena and ground conditions. I believe a properly adjusted tie down contributes to consistent performance and helps a horse maintain a balanced body position.

The term *tie down* doesn't necessarily describe the function. The equipment does more for balance than it does "tying down" a horse's head. I prefer the leather noseband

in the neutral position, as discussed earlier, on the majority of horses I ride. A nylon or rope design is an option if additional control is needed in competition, especially on a horse that is heavy in the rate area. Extreme caution should be taken when riding with tie downs outside the training or competition arena. A horse should never have equipment on his head that restricts his movement when crossing streams or riding in brushy or rough country.

TIP 13 Spurs

Spurs are used for lateral position, not speed. They are used to help the rider place and position the horse's body. You must assume total responsibility and exercise caution if you choose to ride with spurs. Often when a horse rates or turns, the rider accidentally touches the horse with spurs and, in the worst-case scenario, uses the spurs to hang on. This causes frustration and anxiety and shortens the horse's stride, creating bouncy and rough turns. Spurs are not part of the barrel racing costume! If you use them, use them responsibly!

Spur Options:

- ◈ Select a spur with a short one-inch or less downward sloping shank.
- ◈ Use a bumper spur.
- ◈ Use a ball spur without a rowel.
- ◈ Use spurs in training only.
- ◈ Learn to be more effective and responsible with your leg aids.

Keep the rider's toe and heel parallel to the horse's side in order to keep the shank of the spur from touching the horse's side accidentally.

TIP 14 The Whip versus the Over-Under

Any tool is only as good as the rider's ability to use it correctly. The whip may be the most effective tool to increase a horse's stride or drive the horse deeper into the turn; however, it may get in the way of handling the rein or the saddle horn. In untrained hands, a whip can cause a high level of anxiety. In contrast, the over/under remains out of the way on the saddle horn until it is needed. Sometimes it is not as precise as the whip because it can be hard to locate at a high rate of speed. The quirt, carried on the wrist, is an additional tool to drive the horse forward, but it is awkward and, like all aids, requires practice and timing to be effective. Without practice it often throws the rider out of time with the horse. My choice is the over-under. I have it on my saddle horn at all times, for both training and competition.

Caution should be taken not to sit flat, fall back, or pull on the reins when asking the horse to move forward with one of the aids mentioned. Like a jockey, waving the whip or over/under in rhythm with the horse's stride creates additional forward movement and aids in increasing the horse's stride. Using the whip out of rhythm while the horse's front feet are on the ground actually decreases the length of stride. Practice using the whip, over/under, or quirt by riding a saddle over a bale of hay to simulate the rider's position in relation to the horse's movement.

TIP 15 Using the Over-Under

To aid in timing and rhythm, the length of the over/under, whether it is made of rope, leather, or nylon, should fall just above the horse's knee. With the thumb forward and knuckles down, slide your hand halfway down the over/under. An over/under reinforces forward motion, impulsion, and length of stride. The use of the over/under should be preceded with a verbal "kiss" or "cluck." The over/under is used to urge a horse forward, *not* to whip the horse forward. The action of the over/under mimics a waving motion and should be used discreetly in rhythm with the horse's stride. The tool can be used literally from one side of the horse to the other, or can be used on just one side of the horse to reinforce movement. Experiment with different designs to see which weight and style suits you best.

TIP 16 Adjusting the Breast Collar

Depending on the individual horse's conformation and athletic ability, each stride at a gallop takes approximately three-tenths of a second. Any resistance against the point of the horse's shoulder or windpipe caused by a poorly fitted breast collar can shorten the horse's stride or restrict his intake of air, each of which can affect the outcome of a race. Caution should be taken to elevate the breast collar above the points of the horse's shoulder, with the center of the breast collar well below the soft tissue and windpipe in the center of the horse's chest. Feel for the breastplate to center the breast collar and locate the forward point of the horse's shoulder. This can be accomplished in three ways. Elevate the breast collar D to the upper concho on the saddle, use a neck strap to pick up the breast collar, or select a Freedom Fit design from Court's Saddlery.

In today's competition, where one one-thousandth of one second could make a difference in a win, it is important to know how each piece of equipment affects the movements of the horse.

TIP 17 Using the Drop Noseband

The drop noseband can be used on horses that open their mouths to escape the contact of the training snaffle and to remind a young horse in training that opening his mouth is unacceptable. Make sure before you choose to use a drop noseband that your

hands are not too aggressive or abusive. Perhaps most importantly, have your equine dentist make sure your horse is dentally sound. Dental problems could very possibly be the root of many difficulties that horses have with their bits.

Adjust the noseband so two fingers can be inserted between the leather strap and the horse's nose. Anytime you use mouth-shutting aids, remember that a supple jaw leads to a supple horse. Always be cautious in the adjustment of the noseband that you are not inhibiting the movement of the jaw. Place the noseband over the headstall below the bit, as this avoids pinching the corners of the horse's mouth between the bit and the noseband.

The Reinsman drop noseband design I choose can be converted to a cavason when used with leverage bits. The cavason is adjusted to go under the headstall and above the bit. Again, make sure the cavason is adjusted so that is rests high enough off of the bit that it avoids any pinching at the horse's lip.

FOUR

TRAINING TIPS
FOR A BETTER FOUNDATION

Winning is accomplished in the fundamental phase, not the execution phase.

—*Vince Lombardi*

Excellence Comes in the Mastery of Fundamentals

In barrel racing, the mastery of fundamentals comes with a lifetime of commitment, dedication, practice, preparation, and experience, and then you add speed and the learning process begins all over again!

It's not my place to judge, but I do have to question riders' decisions to leave the outcome of a competition to their horse. My weakness or strength in competition came from the decision to sacrifice perhaps three-tenths of a second in exchange for hands-on horsemanship. Call me a control freak, but I always opted for the solid average run *every time*, rather than taking the chance to let it roll for the fastest run *one time*.

It certainly takes courage in the barrel race to throw caution to the wind and gamble on the outcome. The opportunity to make the fastest run or set an arena record requires a "winner take all" mentality. Arguably, I was never a courageous competitor in that sense and yet consistent wins bought gas, paid entry fees, and allowed me to follow my dreams one competition weekend at a time. As a competitor, I lived by the philosophy that every run had to count. Therefore, my strategy was to plan the run and run the plan, which gave me the courage to ride into each competitive condition with a purpose and, most importantly, with a plan. Call it intelligent horsemanship; I just couldn't talk myself into letting my horse, with a brain slightly larger than a walnut, make the ultimate decisions that would determine the outcome of our competition.

The thought of spending hours in the arena training, tuning, scoring, conditioning, and practicing the mental focus necessary to make a precise run, only to release control when my entry fee is on the line and pray that everything would come together during this precise fifteen to seventeen seconds of competition just didn't make sense to me. One mistake—an incorrect pocket position, one shortened stride at the inappropriate time—and I don't get a paycheck for the hard work and effort I invested in the run.

"No guts, no glory" is one motto, but being a winner is not just making a winning run sometimes, it is having the ability to make a qualifying run every time. Don't beat yourself or outrun your ability. These are two of the most difficult lessons to learn when speed comes into play.

Each run is a learning opportunity, a chance to evaluate strengths and weaknesses, and a chance to learn a lesson that makes the next run better than the last. Winning runs are not answers to prayers; they don't come by luck or fate. Winning runs are created through preparation, practice, and experience and come when the opportunity to excel presents itself.

Year after year the top competitors, the recognized and most consistent performers, understand the method of producing consistent performance regardless of the size of arena or ground conditions. Winners expect to win and they take it in stride. Losing is harder to accept and more difficult to live with. Charlie Brown's loyal beagle Snoopy made the famous statement, "Winning isn't everything, until you lose!" The famous football coach Vince Lombardi said, "Winning is accomplished in the fundamental phase, not the execution phase." In the barrel race, the mastery of fundamentals comes from preparation, practice, and experience. Then you add speed and the process begins all over again!

TIP 1 Building Patience and Discipline

Performance horses are athletes. Athletes need discipline. I saddle my horses that are in training for a few hours each day. How long depends on the nature of the horse. Assertive, high-strung horses usually spend longer under the saddle, regardless of the actual riding time. I practice this routine even when I am hauling. Just having my horse stand saddled at the horse trailer does wonders for his mental state of mind and helps build patience and discipline.

TIP 2 Creating the Willing Horse

If a horse does not understand what is expected of him he becomes resistant, anxious, and frustrated. This causes his movements and transitions to be stiff, rough, and difficult at best. Whether it is for training or for competition, it remains the rider's responsibility to create an environment where the horse enjoys his job and remains eager to work. We achieve this goal through patience, preparation, education, and consistent training both in and out of the arena.

TIP 3 **Dr. David Hayes's "One-Step Horsemanship"**

A willing horse taught through praise and understanding works harder, faster, and happier than a horse trained through fear and pain. Here are a few key thoughts while training and riding that help you develop and support a winning athlete.

◈ Keep in mind that lessons are better learned through praise than pain.
◈ Corrections should provide a desire to please rather than flee.
◈ Make your horse your friend, not your slave.
◈ Ask for small steps and be ready to reward the smallest try.
◈ Always look for what your horse is doing right rather than what he may be doing wrong.

◈ Praise makes them willing; fear makes them falter.

◈ A willing athlete runs faster and smarter than a scared or fearful one.

◈ Build a solid foundation today for a solid performance tomorrow.

Dr. Hayes has been my consulting veterinarian and was my number-one pit crew boss when I was on the professional circuit. He stands with my father as possibly my number-one fan today. The shoes he made for my horses were always handmade and balanced. He advocated high fat, low starch nutrition thirty years ago—years before the industry accepted the concept. Dr. Hayes helped develop a conditioning program for the barrel racing discipline. His philosophy is all about the horse. His knowledge is a balance of academics and practical application.

Dr. Hayes, as an advocate of the horse, believes if a person takes on the ownership of a horse then that person takes on the *full responsibility* for that horse. The owner must consider the feeding, the watering, the exercise, the housing, the hoof care, and the health care of his horse, but also the less tangible conditions. It is the owner's responsibility to address the horse's social interactions and his needs as a "herd animal." Dr. Hayes reminds us to consider the fact that a horse has an inherent need for a leader, for mental stimulation, and most importantly, for praise and the reassurance of belonging.

TIP 4 Usefulness of a Well-Constructed and Correctly Fitted Halter

Consider the lead rope and halter as a connection with your horse, similar to the reins. Both are lines of communication. The halter that is most useful for communication is a moderate-sized rope halter that is proportional to your horse's head. The throatlatch needs to fit snugly and be centered under the jaw, the poll strap just behind the ears, and the nosepiece positioned just below the facial crest. When asked to move forward, the halter should lift the nose from behind the jaw, instead of pulling directly on the poll. The lead rope and halter should be balanced in weight and attached with a knot, avoiding any heavy or breakable snap. Swinging snaps confuse the lines of communication. Avoid just "hanging the halter on the head." Rather, put it on like you might need to use it. Be prepared for the unexpected!

TIP 5 Sequencing Cues

Learning to repetitiously sequence cues is essential to mentally and physically prepare the horse for the response the rider is requesting. When asking for results like forward, stop, back, laterals, 360s, and rollbacks, it is necessary to learn and practice consistent cues to help signal to your horse that a request from the rider is on the way. The maneuver begins as a thought in the rider's mind. Cues to the horse begin in the rider's seat and legs, then travel from the rider's hands through the reins and to the horse's mouth. This transfer of information forms the connection between the request and the response within the horse's brain.

The sequencing of cues needs to be clear, crisp, and consistent. Your horse is not a mind reader! This sequence usually involves a series of three commands, starting with the positioning of the rider's body, followed by rein reinforcement, and lastly the connection at the bit. A verbal command can be used after the rider's body position has signaled the horse that a request from the bit is forthcoming. The repetitious sequencing of cues helps create trust and feel between the rider and horse. Often the horse learns to give the rider the requested maneuver at the same time he feels the rider's body cue for response. A reward of immediate release of pressure tells the horse he has done well. The more precisely and clearly the rider teaches and reinforces the sequence of cues in training, the quicker the horse will respond to the rider in competition.

TIP 6 Backing Your Horse with Balance

The exercise of backing contributes to better balance, rate, and stops. It is often a skill that is overlooked and underappreciated. Sure, you say, I can back my horse! I say, OK, can you back in a circle, a zigzag? Can you back until *you* say far enough, or does the horse take a token three steps and stop himself? Pay attention.

Horses learn from reward. So often when our horses give us the token few steps, drop their poll, tuck their chins, and stall their feet, our first response may be to quit asking and release the rein pressure. When we respond this way we tell the horse he "done good!" The fact is that he lost balance, quit moving, and resisted the rider's request.

When you think about backing your horse, first identify what it is you are asking for and be prepared to achieve the requested maneuver. Shorten your reins for connection and sequence your backing cues. As you begin, shift your weight back, anchor your seat bones, and tilt your shoulders back behind your center of gravity. Next, apply leg and request movement. Finally, pick up the reins, slightly offset if the horse is bracing on the bit, and designate the direction in which you want the horse's feet to move. If the horse drops at the poll, shifting his weight forward, lift one rein hand straight up to elevate the horse's poll and shoulder. The other rein hand remains in neutral position and directs the horse in the desired direction. Bump with both calves, not heels, to liven the horse's feet and generate energy.

As the horse rebalances his poll, elevates his shoulder, shifts his weight back, and moves his feet, immediately reward the effort by releasing the rein pressure. Three steps are the foundation that leads to five steps that lead to as many steps as requested by the rider.

If a horse is backing crooked it is because he is not balanced. To correct this issue, focus on the line in which you wish to back. If the horse drifts his hip to the left, he is dropping his right shoulder. Respond by elevating the right rein higher than the left, which is backing the horse, while blocking the incorrect direction with the left calf against the horse's rib at a point towards the back cinch. Regain the straight back and reward the horse's efforts. A horse that can back in an unrestricted movement redistributes his weight behind the cinch. This exercise increases the horse's ability to stop, spin, and roll back.

TIP 7 Using Outside Rein for Rate and Collection

The outside rein not only helps balance the horse's head and body, but, in the barrel race, offers speed control. Learn to support the horse during the approach to each barrel and into the rate with both hands on the rein riding each side of the horse. This is especially important in training the young or green horse and equally important on finished horses that may depend on the rider for support and balance. One of the most crucial areas of any winning run is the last straight stride into the rate point and start of the turn. This takes a knowledgeable and courageous rider with skill and patience to ride into this position without going to the horn too early. It may take two hands to ride into that last full stride before the turn and keep the horse straight, but it can certainly make the difference in an efficient turn and a winning run.

TIP 8   Communication: Is Your Horse Listening to You?

You need to be clear and consistent with your cueing, rewards, and corrections. Horses learn by repetition. There are six basic steps to establish a cue with your horse:

1. Have a mental picture.
2. Give the desired signal or cue.
3. Make the right thing easy, and the wrong thing difficult.
4. Reward the slightest effort.
5. Repeat with consistency.
6. Know when to quit.

Remember that the horse also communicates with us in his own way. Know your horse and know what behavior is normal for him. Recognize when he is trying to tell you something. Communication is necessary in order for the rider and horse to work as a team in the high-adrenaline, high-pressure environment of barrel racing.

TIP 9   Creating Gymnastic Exercises

Learn to be creative in your training and practice. Think about the skills and maneuvers you and your horse need to master in order to run an efficient and consistent pattern. Create opportunities in your daily work to practice those skills to enhance your barrel race. Straight lines are the shortest way to move between two points and are necessary for an efficient approach to each barrel. Incorporate riding straight lines inside and outside the arena. Identify visual aids: trees, fence posts, or cones to help establish your straight lines. This helps you pick points in order to ride consistently into your barrel position.

The approach requires acceleration for the race, and collection or rate necessary to shorten the horse's stride before asking for the turn. Being able to extend the stride at

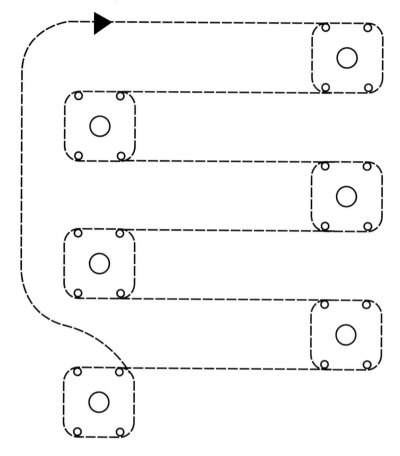

all gaits and collect the stride is an important ingredient to balanced and efficient turns. All exercises take rhythm, forward, and balance. A necessary ingredient is the ability to run a cloverleaf pattern at a high rate of speed making three changes of direction. Create opportunities to work on these skills by incorporating them into effective exercises. Regardless of speed, attention and practice are required to make smooth transitions.

Frequent upward and downward gait transitions, versus prolonged loping, will help with responsiveness. If your horse is pulling you out of the saddle by constantly leaning into the bit, he is out of balance. Typically, conformation puts 65 percent of the horse's weight forward of the cinch. Through training we can redistribute the weight back toward the horse's hind end for better balance and lighter control. Skip a gait if the horse is strong and pulling; for example, lope and then drop to a walk before returning to the lope. Be creative, as there are many opportunities to incorporate exercises and drills into your daily riding program.

The above serpentine pattern, using barrels and cones, is an excellent exercise to develop straight lines, extension, collection, and balance. It provides practice for and helps with the ability to maneuver turns necessary for the barrel pattern.

TIP 10 Creating a Confident and Rider-Focused Horse

Avoid riding on the fence or rail of your arena so your horse does not learn to use it as a crutch. Be attentive to having your horse depend on you for guidance, direction, and confidence. To help promote attention, practice riding the quarter line of your arena. The quarter line is halfway between the rail and the centerline. Diagonal transitions from one corner to the other are good diversions. An occasional trail ride also helps refocus the horse on the rider.

FIVE

BALANCED RIDER— BALANCED HORSE

Riding is a discipline that requires us to be in the moment. Learning to control our mind and body produces successful interaction with our horse.

Attitude

The longer I live and the more people I meet, the more I realize the impact of attitude on life. Attitude is more important than facts. It is more important than the past, than education, than money, than circumstances, than failures, than success, than what other people think or say or do. Attitude is more important than appearance, giftedness, or skill. Attitude makes or breaks a company or a home. The remarkable thing is that we have a choice regarding the attitude we embrace for the day. We cannot change the past. We cannot change the fact that people act in a certain way. We cannot change the inevitable. The only thing we can do is cultivate our attitude.

My young friend Kalyn Brooks understood that life is 10 percent what happens and 90 percent how you react. Kalyn was born with physical handicaps, including a cleft palate, deformed hands, and deficient growth hormones. Kalyn was also deaf and never "heard" that she could not excel in the things she loved to do.

Kalyn loved to ride. Her horses were her mobility and a way to escape her physical challenges. Kalyn was one of the best students I ever taught. She never heard a word I said, yet she never missed a point I made. She watched and emulated demonstrations, read instructional material, watched DVDs, and took to heart the evaluations we made of her riding techniques.

She went on to win many regional championships, rodeo queen contests, and academic awards. Kalyn won the 2000 Sharon Camarillo Western Classic 4D Championship. Though Kalyn always expected to win, she was never disappointed when she did not. Kalyn was rewarded by accomplishing the task that she had set out to do.

Kalyn passed away at the age of twenty-three. She asked her mother, Penny, to go to the arena with her so she could work her horse, Makka. After a perfect performance, and a sprint home from the third barrel, the angels met Kalyn to carry her across the finish line.

Kalyn embraced attitude every day of her life. Here is just a sample of the lifetime lessons Kalyn left us with:

Adversity: Ignore it!

Achievement: Lay the plan and wait for the chance.

Loving: Don't hesitate to show someone you care. Most importantly, love life.

Shopping: If you like it, buy it. There is no such thing of having too much of what you really like.

Joy: Have joy in your spirit and share it. It's contagious.

Food: Eat from the bottom of the food pyramid.

Horses: Ride the ones you like no matter what anyone says, and have enough sense to stay off of the goofy ones.

Clothes: One can never have too much leopard, purple, fringe, red, white, and blue, or sequins. Be brave enough to wear what you like.

Pageantry: Ride Palominos whenever possible and always carry a flag.

Doing the Impossible: Try it.

Helping Others: Help whenever possible, in whatever way.

Negativity: Pretend you are deaf and don't listen.

Dancing: Do it, even if you can't hear the music.
Dogs: Train them.
Dreams: Always have one.
Angels: Believe in them.

Kalyn lived as she believed. She was happy; took the time to share; was brave, silly, thoughtful; allowed herself to be loved; and loved fiercely in return. She never wasted a day and she excelled in her endeavors. For her attitude and cowgirl spirit, Kalyn was inducted posthumously into the National Cowgirl Museum and Hall of Fame in 2007. Kalyn left her footprints on every one she met. Her story will continue to be told, reminding each of us to believe in ourselves, that all things are possible, and to imagine the possibilities.

Balanced and Relaxed Riders Create Balanced and Relaxed Horses

Unbalanced riders are not able to consistently balance or repetitiously cue horses. Tense muscles create stiff joints in the riders and that tenseness transfers to the horse resulting in rough, shortened gaits, poor transitions, and loss of fluid stride and forward momentum. Stiff riders create stiff horses. Relaxed riders create relaxed horses. Horses are the mirror image of their rider's ability. It is important to remember to ride, and more important to practice riding, with soft limbs and joints. A relaxed pelvis acts as a shock absorber between the footfalls of the horse hitting the ground and the rider's upper body. If you find yourself bouncing out of the saddle, slow the horse down and regain rhythm and softness. A soft pelvis will also enhance the quality and smoothness of gaits.

TIP 2 Balanced Rider

How balanced are you when riding? This is where a video camera is a useful training aid. The camera never lies and does not argue! Your shoulder, hip, and heel should be in alignment. Posture is important from the ground up. A rider that walks balanced with good posture has an easier time translating good posture to his riding. Softened shoulders and tight stomach muscles help riders connect their seat to the saddle. Ride from your core and remember that your center of balance is just below your belt buckle. It is important when a horse makes a move, that the rider remains soft and supple in order to follow the motion of the horse, and more important, especially when speed is added,

that the rider is neither ahead nor behind that move. Riding balanced builds the horse's confidence and helps establish the seamless transitions that are so important in a fast, money-making run.

TIP 3 Balanced Horse

A balanced moving horse is one who moves with more than half of his bodyweight distributed behind the cinch towards his haunches. Balanced horses are easier to train, smoother and safer to ride, stay sound longer, and are more athletic. In order for the competitive horse to work as quickly and efficiently as possible we must teach and insist that they maintain balanced movement. Sixty-five percent of the horse's body weight is naturally carried from the cinch forward. Through training we are able to redistribute

and balance the horse enabling him to elevate his front end for athletic movement and increase his impulsion from behind.

TIP 4 Rhythm

Incorporate rhythm in your work. If you have difficulty having a smooth and consistent practice, generally it is because the horse has lost his rhythm. Reestablish the horse forward and with rhythm, at a sitting trot, extended trot, or lope before returning to your exercise. Rhythm is a necessary component of every gait. Refer to the training pyramid in Chapter 10 to see that establishing "rhythm" is the foundation to effective training, warm-up, and consistent competition.

Never abuse the horse by jerking the reins, causing damage to the horse's bars and tongue.

TIP 5

Exercises to Improve the Rider's Body Position, Balance, and Timing

- Gymnastic exercises
- Lunge line lessons
- Stopping without pulling on reins
- Sitting trot with rhythm and balance
- Extended trot with rhythm and balance
- Trot in the two point or half-seat position
- Ride without stirrups
- Post without stirrups

TIP 6 The Importance of Diagonals

The term "diagonal" in relation to a trot is the same as a "lead" is to define a balanced lope or canter. The trot is a diagonal two-beat gait with the horse using his legs in diagonal pairs. For example, the right fore and left hind leg leave the ground together, and then the left fore and right hind follow, making a two-beat rhythm. Sit at the jog, extend your trot when in posting position. Correct diagonals should be used at the extended trot. To help remember which diagonal is correct, I apply this simple rhyme: "Rise and fall with the horse's fore leg nearest the wall." This is an easy way to remember to rise to the outside leg, as the horse's diagonal inside hind leg lifts you out of the saddle.

TIP 7 Leads

"Lope" and "canter" are interchangeable terms. Usually the lope is associated with western riding. Leads associated to the gait have a three-beat rhythm controlled by the rider. To the left, the horse brings his right hind leg under and pushes off, the left hind and right fore hit the ground at the same time and then the left fore hits the ground and

carries all the horse's weight, for a brief period of time, as he rolls forward over it. All four feet are in the air for a split second until the right hind moves forward to repeat the cycle. Correct leads in the approach and turn are associated with balanced and efficient performance and aid in smooth, fast turns.

Teach the horse to start the race and hold the turning lead to and around the first barrel. Teach the horse through simple lead transitions to change leads two or so strides after the first turn. The horse should hold the correct lead to, and around, the second barrel and into and around the third barrel. It takes time to change leads, however once the horse turns the third barrel, I am not concerned which lead the horse runs across the finish line in.

TIP 8 The Gallop

The gallop is not a fast lope; it is the fourth gait, following the walk, trot, and lope or canter. It is a four-beat gait. The gallop has a similar sequence as the lope; however, the diagonal pair no longer hit the ground simultaneously. There is a period of suspension where all four feet are off the ground at the same time.

TIP 9 **Practice Perfect**

Practice perfect for better performance. Remember, whatever minor or major problems you feel developing in your practice work will be magnified in your run. I believe you should practice perfect for better performance and take the time to correct developing problems, no matter how insignificant they seem in the practice pen. This philosophy helps keep the horse honest and helps develop muscle memory in the rider. Any stiffness in the horse's body should be addressed, and varying speed in all gaits should be incorporated in practice. Learning to practice with speed is ultimately important so that the horse learns to accept the increased pressure that is required in competition. A rider has approximately five seconds to make a correction once a mistake is identified before the horse commits the response to memory and assumes it to be what the rider is asking for.

Perfection is the goal in practice. Remember to reward the slightest effort on behalf of the horse and that "Rome was not built in a day." Consistency in reward and discipline is essential in developing consistent performance.

TIP 10 Personal Fitness for the Rider

The more integrity that riders can maintain in their personal carriage and posture, the more balance they will bring to their horses. A rider needs aerobic conditioning, Yoga for suppleness and stretching, weight training for core strengthening, and weight and nutritional management. These are all valuable skills that contribute to effective

riding. There are some great books available that focus on these skills. All disciplines address using these areas to strengthen discipline-specific riding, especially for the serious rider and competitor. We spend time on horse care and the conditioning of our equine athletes, often at the expense of ignoring the same considerations necessary for a balanced, focused, nutritionally sound, and conditioned rider.

Mental focus, physical fitness, and a positive attitude all go hand in hand as we work toward mastering our event-specific skills.

TIP 11 Ride with Purpose

Success is a lifestyle. Before stepping in the stirrup, identify what it is you expect to achieve in each ride, be it relaxation, conditioning, training, or a tune-up. Learn to identify the mental and physical condition of your horse. Identify his strengths and weaknesses. Identify your personal strengths and weaknesses. Though each ride may not result in perfection, each ride is an opportunity to strengthen both your skills and your horse's skills. Learn to ride not as a passenger but as an active participant working toward a successful outcome.

Avoid stopping to make a correction, unless it is for rate. Use legs and/or the end of rein or over/under to maintain impulsion and forward motion. Corrections need forward motion and impulsion to be effective.

TIP 12 Adjusting Stirrup Length for Better Performance

After watching students make their introductory barrel runs, one of the most common suggestions I make at each clinic is to check stirrup length. I find that many riders' stirrups are one hole too long. Arena riding requires technical maneuvers that are easier to accomplish with proper and balanced stirrup length.

The easiest way for me to adjust stirrup length is to have the rider place their foot in the stirrup exactly how they will be riding, stand in the stirrups with a flat foot, with the toe and heel level to the ground, and with slightly bent knees. This should produce a two- to three-finger distance between the inseam of the jeans and the saddle seat. Many factors influence stirrup length, including the type of boot worn by the rider. Crepe soles, thin soles, and flat soles all influence the adjustment, and should be considered each time you climb into the saddle. Proper stirrup length helps maintain a rider's balance and position. With this said, I certainly recommend dropping stirrups for trail or ranch riding. Balance is critical, since a balanced rider is crucial to a balanced horse.

Remember to embrace a positive attitude everyday with open arms. Life offers many lessons; learn them well.

SIX

Simple Exercises for Better Barrel Racing

Learn to enjoy the journey. Life is a succession of events that interlock for success.

Enjoying the Journey

"It is not the critic who counts; not the man who points out how the strong man stumbles or where the doer of deeds could have done better. The credit belongs to the man who is actually in the arena, whose face is marred by dust and sweat and blood, who strives valiantly, who errs and comes up short again and again because there is not effort without error or shortcoming, but who know the great enthusiasm, the great devotions, who spends himself for a worthy cause; who, at the best, knows, in the end, the triumph of high achievement, and who, at the worst, if he fails, at least he fails while daring greatly, so that his place shall never be with those cold and timid souls who knew neither victory or defeat."

—Theodore Roosevelt

TIP 1 Five Important Parts of the Horse

For the sake of education and identification, I concentrate on five specific parts of the horse in training and competition. These areas translate to balance and position, and help in performance evaluation. Lack of control in any one of these areas can significantly influence efficient performance and effective training. The concept of seeing the horse as five parts comes from Les Vogt's training video, *Five Easy Pieces.*

1. The head/neck
2. The shoulder
3. The rib cage
4. The hip
5. The feet

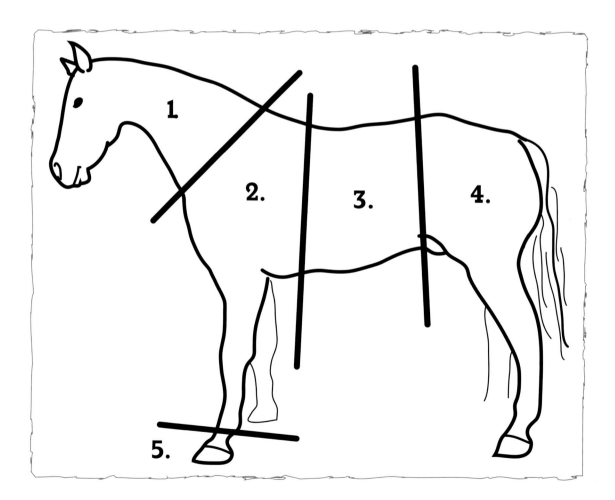

Since we want the finished horse to use all five parts in concert with one another, we need to be able to isolate each part to properly understand its function. Through various exercises we teach the horse to move in coordinated balance and alignment so we can quickly and efficiently correct his body at speed to ensure the balanced movement needed for a fast efficient run. As I ride, I have to remember the words of the late Ray Hunt: "First we have to learn how to control the parts of the horse before we can ride the whole."

TIP 2 Riding the Squared Circle

Establish a visual circle in the riding area and imagine the four quarters or corners of the circle.

When trotting, loping, or galloping the circle, ride four straight lines on the squared circle and connect with four soft, semi-round corners. It helps to ride the squared circle with both hands on the reins to help balance both sides of the horse's shoulders and ribs. The goal: connect the rider's seat—ride so that the horse is balanced in-between the rider's hands and leg aids. The concept of the squared circle helps the horse travel in a perfect circle without leaning in or drifting out. The rhythm of riding to "points," or corners on the circle, helps the barrel racer ride to modified points on the barrel pattern. Again, the skills reinforce visual aids that help plan the direction in which one is riding, and to travel in the established direction with a connected seat, soft

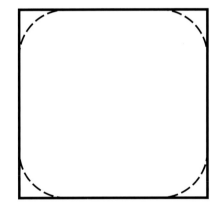

leg aids, and connected reins. This puts into action the precept that you should plan the ride and ride the plan. In the sport of barrel racing, this statement is modified to, "Plan the Run, Run the Plan!"

TIP 3 Shoulder-In/Shoulder-Out Exercise

A gymnastic exercise that is easy to accomplish in most settings is shoulder-in/shoulder-out. This exercise is done at a jog or lope in a large, neutral circle. The exercise:
◈ Teaches the horse to move his shoulders to the inside or outside of a circle
◈ Teaches the horse to move off leg and rein pressure

◈ Gives the rider the ability to pick up a horse's shoulder during a run if the horse fades or drops toward a barrel

◈ Incorporates increased bending of the inside hind leg which is required for turns

◈ Tests responsiveness of horse and rider's timing and coordination of seat, leg, and rein aids

◈ Provides effective ways to improve suppleness

◈ Is an effective exercise to diffuse performance anxiety in the warm-up area

To implement the shoulder-in/shoulder-out exercise, visually establish a large squared circle in the riding area approximately fifty feet in diameter. Make sure that the horse is well-framed, relaxed, and balanced between your hands before you begin any training skill. Perform the exercise in a four-count cue sequence:

1. Shift rider's weight into the outside stirrup
2. Release the pressure of the outside rein.
3. Roll the inside wrist, palm up, to elevate the horse's inside shoulder.
4. Elevate the hand, straighten the elbow and move the rein hand up the horse's neck toward the horse's ear until the horse's nose tips in and the outside shoulder moves to the outside of the circle.

Take care not to cross the rein over the mane to the opposite side of the horse. Also remember that the more slowly you cue, the more quickly the horse learns to respond. The horse should eventually maintain the shoulder-in/shoulder-out position for ten to fifteen strides. Once the horse is proficient at the jog, perform the exercise at a lope while working to achieve the same results.

Reward the slightest effort, especially on a young or green horse. Finish the exercise by returning to the neutral position on the circle and move into the next choreographed skill exercise.

TIP 4 Lengthen and Shorten Exercise

Regardless of the warm-up area available, you can always make sure you have the ability to adjust speed within each gait. If circumstances allow only for walking or trotting, adjust the horse's walking stride by variegating the walking speed. Adjust the trot by alternating the sitting trot with the extended trot. At a lope, make sure to gallop the horse out, then sit and ask the horse to shorten his stride back to a slower lope. The more easily a horse can adjust his speed, the more responsive he will become when you ask for a rate on the barrel pattern.

This skill becomes extremely valuable when asking the horse to rate his barrel in preparation for a balanced and quick turn. The skill is taught and practiced at all levels

of training and leads to accurate and precise collection and rate during the barrel run. In Chapter 10, the training pyramid helps explain how this ability builds on the raw athletic skills necessary for efficient performance.

TIP 5 Circle on a Circle Exercise

This exercise has been designed to complement the skills necessary to make a balanced approach, successfully shorten the stride for rate, and incorporate precisely placed barrel turns. In your mind's eye, identify a fifty foot circle. Imagine a clock face. Now, identify the twelve o'clock position, nine o'clock position, six o'clock position, and three o'clock position on four quarters of the circle. Pretend there is a barrel sitting on each number. Lope the large circle until the horse is traveling in a relaxed way and is balanced in-between your reins while maintaining a rhythmic gait. Sit in the saddle and apply rein rate at the imaginary twelve, nine, six, or three o'clock position; hold the forward one stride to allow the horse to gain collection for the turn. Incorporate a smaller circle using the direct rein for direction and the indirect rein to help support the outside shoulder under the horse. Return to the larger circle. Ride the larger circle until the horse regains a relaxed and rhythmic gait before repeating the exercise. Remember to use consistent and repetitious cues by sitting first and using outside rein for rate and speed control before asking for the smaller circle.

TIP 6 Scoring Performance Horses for Confidence and Relaxation

Scoring is the process of not only riding towards the first barrel in a relaxed and rewarding manner, but includes riding in and out of the alleyway or arena gate. Allow your horse to move into the arena toward the first barrel while calmly talking or petting

the anxious horse. Persuade the horse to relax and walk with flat feet to help gain confidence and focus his attention on you, the rider. The key here is that the rider must also work on being relaxed in order to transfer this emotion to the horse. Relax, pet, turn around, and ride back out of the gate and repeat, and repeat. Reward the horse's attention by stopping, backing up, stepping off the horse, and loosening the cinch before turning away from the pattern and out of the arena. This teaches your horse that the gate is not a bad place to be and helps to relieve performance anxiety upon entering the arena.

TIP 7 Cross Training

Let's face it: three stationary barrels in the same place all the time can get boring. Anxiety and frustration are by-products of too much pattern work. Be creative in finding ways to enhance your horse's abilities off the pattern or outside the arena. Go on some trail rides. Outside riding helps get the horse refocused on the rider instead of depending on arena fences and training drills for response. There are many creative ways out on the trail to work on a multitude of skills like extension and collection, supplementing, conditioning, and relaxation. Working or roping cattle, or even following a flag—similar to the technique used by cutting horse trainers—can help develop your horse's quickness and coordination while keeping him interested. Learn some reining or dressage exercises to help your horse develop his top line and balance. Be creative and keep it fun! The barrel race is about straight lines, lengthening and shortening of stride for speed control, and balance in directional changes. There are many opportunities for the rider to enhance these skills away from the barrel pattern.

SEVEN

STRATEGIES FOR MAKING A COMPETITION RUN

Excellence in performance begins with a vision of where you want to go, then establishing goals to get there.

A Week in the Life of a Professional Barrel Racer

The task of keeping seasoned performance horses in peak condition is different from training and seasoning young horses. Even a finished horse will have flaws that need to be corrected, but proper training should give the horse the foundation necessary to correct and repair the majority of performance faults. As expensive as it is today to haul in any competitive venue, efficiency and consistent performance is mandatory.

Therefore, any rider on the professional level should also have the evaluation skills necessary to identify both rider and horse's strengths and weaknesses in order to maintain consistent winning performance.

Once these strengths and weaknesses have been identified, a plan needs to be implemented after each competition to locate a facility to use for retraining or the correction necessary to prepare for the next competition. This is sometimes difficult when on the road. This concept is similar to the NASCAR race circuit. Between races the team and driver identify those areas that are helping or hindering their effort to reach the winner's circle. Usually before they leave a race they use the track to make necessary changes to the car to ready it for the next race. Changes are immediately implemented to complement good performance or modify and correct poor performance. I live by the rule, "Unless I win I cannot stay on the road." I need to be prepared to make each and every run count.

The finished performance horse needs to be conditioned, and good nutrition needs to be maintained for peak performance. The better physical condition the horse is in, the less risk we run of incurring injuries from inconsistency in ground conditions or lack of preparation.

A good horse deserves good attention and a consistent schedule. Each day revolves around feeding, exercising, and tune-ups. I usually take Monday off after a weekend competition. A day in the sun and pasture, or just relaxing in an outdoor pen is a nice way to relax and work out tight muscles. It is also a great way to relax a horse mentally.

Tuesday is usually a light training day with the primary focus placed on a conditioning routine. At least three days per week, I plan on riding to maintain the condition necessary for peak performance. It takes a minimum of five miles to produce visible results from conditioning. One mile at a walk to loosen and relax muscles, one mile at an extended trot to tighten stomach muscles and work on length of stride, and one mile or perhaps two at a gallop, depending on the horse. The gallop is a great way to increase lung capacity and wind, as well as to improve strength and muscle tone. The gallop is faster than the lope. You need to maintain an extension in stride for it to be useful.

The conditioning exercises should be done outside the arena if possible. If an arena is the only or the safest area to ride, use the walk to loosen and relax muscles. Long trot down the long side of the arena, collect the stride and maintain a collected trot or jog on the shorter side of the arena before extending the stride back down the long side of the arena. Calculate at least a mile at the trot. Add a lope or gallop for approximately five to seven minutes in order to build and maintain lung capacity for maximum performance in most timed events.

Always remember to finish any condition exercise with a complete and thorough walking cool out. This could take up to two miles. It is at this time that I go back to gymnastic exercises designed to enhance performance and correct performance faults.

Wednesday and Thursday before weekend performance are used to continue conditioning exercises and event-specific corrections. Afternoon baths and turn out is a great way to relax and refresh horses' minds and bodies. I have even looked for a stream if I cannot find a pasture for relaxation. It feels great to let that cold water run up to the knees or even deeper if safe conditions apply.

Performance horses are athletes. Athletes are disciplined. I usually saddle any performance horse for a few hours each day. How long depends on the nature of the horse. Assertive, high-strung horses usually spend a longer time under saddle each day. Even if I am on the road, just having my horse stand saddled at the horse trailer does wonders for his state of mind.

Feeding a consistent quality of hay and grain on schedule is important. Remember, a horse can drink up to 10 gallons of water during stall rest at night, especially in the summer. Make sure when on the road that you haul enough buckets to accommodate your horse's needs. Include table salt in the horse's daily diet to help keep him hydrated. I prefer the addition of loose salt and trace minerals to the use of electrolytes. However, extreme conditions call for extreme measures. If you have any questions consult your veterinarian for the best source to successful nutrition.

TIP 1 Plan the Run, Run the Plan

Once your entry fees are paid, the competitor's goal is to win. However, that winning run takes preparation, planning, and a little luck, too. It is often said that luck is where preparation meets opportunity. There is a direct relation between successful physical and mental training and consistent competition. Some champions have an innate understanding of the connection; others use sports psychology to enhance their understanding. Two excellent resources are: *In Pursuit of Excellence: How to Win in Sport and Life Through Mental Training*, by Terry Orlick, PhD, and *Where There Is a Will There Is a Way*, by James Will, PhD, which is available on www.sharoncamarillo.com.

It remains the responsibility of the rider and trainers to make sure that the horse is conditioned, trained, given a healthy diet, and kept mentally focused. The horse and rider must perform as a team, but the ultimate responsibility rests on the rider's focus and competitive plan for success.

TIP 2 Don't Change the Rules

Quite often we spend our time at home going slowly and showing our horses what we want them to do and how we want them to work. When we get to a barrel race, the excitement and adrenaline take over. People are watching and cheering, and we become overly concerned with the run portion of our race. We forget about cueing and timing, resort to kicking and whipping, and hope for the best. Remember to keep the rules the same in competition as they are in the practice pen. Cue your horse the same way and remember to work as a team. Don't forget to incorporate fast runs at home so the rider and horse can learn how to handle the speed away from the pressure of competition.

TIP 3   Be Creative in Your Pre-Race Warm-Up

A challenge you confront on the competitive trail, traveling from one competition to another, is warm-up areas that are, to be charitable, less than stellar. It is helpful to have a plan in place to address this. You want to ensure that your warm-up can effectively prepare you and your horse for the competition. If you are hauling a short distance to your competition and realize there is a limited warm-up area, one solution may be to ride and lope out before you leave the stabling area and hold your final preparation until you arrive on the grounds. Be a part of the solution and avoid being a part of the problem. Be creative!

TIP 4 **Warm-Up Routines for Competition**

An effective warm-up routine is important for two reasons. First, to get your horse physically warmed up, and second, to get your horse mentally warmed up. Conditions change depending on the race facility, ground conditions, and even the weather. You should also vary your warm-up. Warm up mentally according to your horse's attitude that day. Physically, it takes at least twenty-five minutes, sometimes more depending on the weather, for tendons, ligaments, and muscles to warm up and relax. Ninety percent of your warm-up is done at the walk. The remainder should be a combination of extended and collected trotting and loping in both leads. Finally, make sure to incorporate sprints and collection onto the warm-up routine. It is not always easy in warm-up areas to find the room to sprint; however, it is extremely important to prepare the horse mentally and physically to perform up to his ability and to the rider's expectations. Remember to ride balanced, ride the horse with contact and collection, and maintain rhythm in the gait selected

After the warm-up, check equipment, reset the saddle if necessary, and take time to go over the game plan one more time. Now is the time to determine the effective rein length for the competition run. Remember, as a horse enters the arena to run, his head goes up and all of a sudden the reins may seem too long. Take this into consideration

before you enter the arena, and shorten the reins if necessary. A good rule of thumb is to mechanically place your horse's head in the elevated position that he takes when entering the arena and adjust the reins to just touch the saddle horn. After the run evaluate the adjustment and determine if it was correct. Remember to make a mental note about the adjustment for future runs.

TIP 5 Incorporating Flex into Your Warm-Up

Our horses are athletes and need to be stretched and flexed during warm-up. Think of any athlete. Before the athlete performs or competes, he spends a good amount of time warming up and stretching muscles. Lateral flexing and bending are important for our equine athletes, especially for horses who are naturally stiff. This ensures that his body can take the rigors of a fast run with less chance of injury. Also, spending time to stretch and flex during the warm-up helps the horse be much more responsive, both physically and mentally, during a fast and pressure-filled run.

TIP 6   Picking Points

One of the most important exercises that contribute to consistent performance is to establish visual points in the competition arena that aid in riding a consistent pattern.

First, determine if you are entering the race from a side gate or alleyway. If it is a center approach, the rider needs to decide whether to ride down the left, right, or center. If it is a side gate, decide how far you need to ride across the arena before turning toward the first barrel. Your "start" point establishes your angle of approach into the first barrel. This is very critical because an effective first barrel sets the pace and rhythm for the entire race. If this barrel is smooth, the run flows; if it is rough, the rider plays catch-up into and around the next two barrels.

Establish the "pocket" points into the first, second, and third barrel. It is helpful to establish visual landmarks that remind you where to focus your eyes in order to ride the horse's feet up into rate and turn position. Straight-line approaches to each pocket or turning point are critical for fast times as the shortest distance between two points is a straight line.

Choosing the perfect approach and rate point for each barrel is tricky at best and requires perfect practice during training. Sometimes even the most experienced rider loses focus and lets the horse drift out of position. Remember to establish your points, then look straight beyond that point to the fence or another visual aid. The barrel doesn't move, so learn to keep it in your peripheral vision with your eyes focused on the points you have selected for the response you expect. This skill helps you maintain an upright, balanced approach and an accurate rate. It takes the responsibility off your horse and helps keep him honest and responsively listening to you. Always remain aware of your leg and rein position.

Identify ground conditions and establish "rate" points accordingly. Rate points also depend on the athletic ability and the amount of training of the horse you are riding. Remember, the logistics of the pattern influence rate points. The closer the second and third barrels are to the fence, the deeper the rate point.

TIP 7 Factoring Ground Conditions into Your Run

One of the challenges of barrel racing is dealing with a variety of ground and arena conditions. When warming up, it is always good to introduce your horse to the logistics of the arena, and to get a feel for the ground. If that is not possible, walk in the arena and get a feel for the depth and consistency of the ground and the location of

the course. It is a good idea to watch the other events to see how the horses handle the ground, especially when turning and accelerating.

When warming up for your run look for a place that has similar footing to perform at least some of your ground-specific warm-up exercises. This helps introduce your horse to the conditions. A knowledgeable rider with a horse that is well broke and responsive to modifications can actually use poor ground conditions to gain advantage!

TIP 8   Preparing for a Run on Hard, Shallow, or Slippery Ground

Leverage bits that give more front to back control and less lateral, combined with a tie down or brow band, help keep the horse upright and balanced over his feet.

Warm-up drills for hard ground should focus on straight rate. Warm up by lengthening and shortening the stride on straight lines. Be sure to sequence your rate and stop cues using two hands. Emphasize rate by sitting with a deep seat while applying leg, driving your horse collected into a stop and back. If the horse backs crooked (a sign of a dropped shoulder), add a rollback or series of turnarounds into the direction that the hip moved to rebalance the horse. A balanced horse has an advantage in competition on poor ground.

TIP 9 Horsemanship Strategies for Running on Hard, Shallow, or Slippery Ground

Be sure to start your approach with your horse upright and balanced in-between your hands. Make sure that you are staying upright and balanced in *your* position as well. Use your inside leg to bump, and bump twice to shape the horse's rib if you feel your horse leaning in before the rate. Sit down deep in the saddle at your rate point as you need to rate harder than you would on normal or deep ground. Try to stay two-

handed through the rate, using the outside rein for brake and balance. If the ground is extremely slippery, consider staying two-handed through the turn. If you go to the horn, get two handed again as soon as possible. Ride the rest of the run the same way. Remember to stay straight as you ask for stop at the finish of your run.

TIP 10 **Preparing for a Run on Deep or Heavy Ground**

Choose equipment that keeps your horse free and moving forward, especially if it is a large pattern. In deep ground conditions consider letting out the curb strap; readjusting the tie down, if you use one, to a looser position; or perhaps select a bridle that offers less control. Herein lays the importance of having bridle options.

Warm-up drills for this type of ground focus on getting the horse's feet moving. Warm up by lengthening the stride at the trot, sit down and rate a stride or two, and then work circles, keeping the horse in the bridle while clucking with your voice and bumping with your legs to get the horse's feet driving through the circles. You may want to tap or quietly chase the hip with an over and under to make sure it is free and stepping forward. Leave the circles in a straight line while lengthening the stride, then repeat going both directions. This encourages the horse to drive with his feet through the turn.

A wise competitor always maintains the advantage.

TIP 11 Horsemanship Strategies for Deep or Heavy Ground

Start the approach balanced and straight. Build speed and length of stride from the hind end forward. Remember that the momentum of the approach creates energy in the turn. You need to be accurate with your rate and pocket points. Be cautious not to rate too early or too hard. As soon as you feel your horse shorten his stride, start bumping with your legs to help keep his feet moving through the turn. If the second barrel is close to the fence, drive deep into the rate point and bump and cluck through the turn. Riding toward the third barrel is often the most difficult. With two barrels behind us, we begin to quit thinking, which results in a poorly executed approach and rate position into the third barrel. Once I turn the second barrel, I remind myself to continue running the plan until I cross the finish line.

TIP 12 **Visualizing the Run**

Look around the arena and map out the straight lines for the approach, rate points, and pockets in relationship to the barrels or stakes. If you can, walk the pattern on foot. If not, then walk around the outside of the arena, stopping behind each barrel or stake, visualizing your path. Make mental notes of points on the fence to look toward for your next line of vision when finishing each barrel. Figure out the number of strides you plan to ride between the barrels before your next rate point. Count out each stride in your head. For instance if you determine it is 8 strides between the first and second barrel count out 1, 2, 3, and so on all the way to 8. Think: rate, ride the turn, and finish. Repeat the thought for the third barrel, going through the same process. Be sure to identify the score line and complete your run in your head by riding all the way through and then stopping, balanced and straight. Find a quiet place and mentally make several runs in your head. It is amazing how this exercise can program your body to help your horse have an efficient, rhythmic run. Learn to plan the run and run the plan!

TIP 13 **Alleyway Tips**

As you wait to make a run, one way to stay calm and control your level of anxiety is to focus on your breathing for a few minutes. Take a deep, slow breath, filling your lungs all the way down into your lower rib cage. Count to four and then exhale just as deeply and thoroughly as you inhaled. Repeat this breathing exercise three or four times. This helps calm and relax you while giving you the oxygen you need to ride.

TIP 14 Keeping Your Horse Calm in the Holding Area

Small changes in your body position send signals to the horse that it is time to make a run. While you are waiting to run, stay relaxed and calm in your body position and arms. Be aware of the amount of downward pressure your feet make in the stirrups, keep light contact on the balls of your feet, relaxing your toes, ankles, and knees. Try to keep one hand on the reins in a neutral reining position. Reach back and pet your horse on the hip with your other hand. Repeat this action many times so the horse knows there is a time to relax and stay calm on a loose rein. When it is time to run, establish and maintain forward momentum at the walk or jog into the start position and then gather your reins, set your hands, and put weight down into the stirrups as the horse carries you forward into the run.

Find a song that has a snappy upbeat rhythm that matches the rhythm of your horse's stride. Have that song in your head as you head down the alleyway, it helps with flow and rhythm in your riding.

TIP 15 Tips for Training Alleyway Confidence

After a run, you need to remember that your horse is not completely finished. Beginning the cool out regimen before coming back to the gate or alleyway helps the horse remember he has a job, and it is not only about running barrels. Step off at the gate area, loosen the girth, and take off the leg protection. This teaches the horse that the gate or alley is also a good place and represents more than a position of anxiety. Horses that have moderate to severe gate issues improve by performing workouts designed to apply pressure after the run and then

finish at the gate or alleyway. Be creative when doing this. Act as if you are going to make another run and then finish up the scoring exercise by getting off in the alley or at the gate. Remember, un-cinching is a great way to say, "Well done!"

TIP 16
Tips for Maintaining Body Control and Forward Motion in the Alleyway

Lateral maneuvers are the key to maintaining forward motion and body control under pressure. If the horse locks up, work one side at a time by using lateral aids (for example, left rein back toward the cantle while bumping with your left leg at the rib and flank). Once the horse breaks loose (starts moving the feet), do the double down exercise in that direction. Stand the horse up straight and continue forward and then go in the opposite direction. Other maneuvers to work on at the gate include side-passing, arc and reverse arc, leg yields, and spins. Experiment by starting the maneuvers to the left if you run right. This helps improve your horse's listening skills as well. The ability for the rider to maintain body position is also critical in establishing the correct lead toward the barrel. Inside rein contact and outside leg pressure helps ensure correct lead departures.

TIP 17 Approaching the Barrel Pattern

Correct leads, the line of approach, and the rate point establish well-balanced and efficient turns. Pocket points are a personal decision and the amount of pocket depends on the athletic ability and the stage of training of the horse you are riding. Remember, the quickest way between two points is a straight line. The approach is a straight line between the start point and the first barrel, from the finish point on the first barrel to the pocket point on the second barrel, and from the finish point on the second

barrel to the third barrel pocket point. The line from the finish point on the third barrel across the finish line is straight and strong. To ride a straight line, it may take one hand on each side of the rein to balance, guide, and support the horse. Set your seat bones evenly and light in the saddle seat with a forward sloping pelvis to encourage stride and forward motion. Practice keeping your eyes focused on the pocket and approach points to encourage your horse to remain on the designated line of approach. The barrel itself should only be seen in your peripheral vision. Trust your pattern. The barrels are not moving targets!

TIP 18 The Rate

Once the line of approach and the pocket points are established for the barrel race, the importance of sequencing rate comes into play. This cue or command helps the horse shorten his stride in preparation for a quick and balanced turn. Do not place this responsibility, or choice, solely on your horse's decision. Rate points can change depending on the athletic ability and the degree of training of the horse you are riding. This rate point can also vary depending on the ground and arena conditions. In deep, heavy ground, in order to maintain momentum in the turn, the rate point may be requested closer toward the barrel or even into the turn.

Because of the close proximity to the fence, the second barrel rate should be established closer to the second barrel. Keep two hands on reins, positioned off center to achieve a straight and balanced turn, as the horse is still straight in his approach position. The rider implements the rate command by softening and rounding the pelvis and planting even seat bones in the saddle. Adding leg pressure on a horse that has a tendency to lose forward helps drive the horse through the turn. While the inside rein has directional contact, use of the outside rein helps stabilize the outside shoulder and sets up a balanced turn. The outside rein also signals the inside hock to reach forward.

Rate is the most misunderstood element of barrel racing. This is where the horse is set up for his turn. Rate is not a stop; it requires timing and balance on the part of the rider. Remember that the outside rein is the important element to hold the horse straight until the rate is accomplished. The outside rein is the speed control and also helps establish the size and balance of the turn.

TIP 19

Common Errors in the Rate

◈ Poor selection of rate point
◈ Failure to keep the horse straight until the horse rates
◈ Rating one-handed
◈ Overuse of the inside or outside rein
◈ Poor response to the request for rate
◈ Ineffective cue sequence causing the horse to brace against the rider
◈ Lack of education or understanding of the importance of the outside rein
◈ Loss of impulsion
◈ Sitting or going to the horn too early before the rate or turn
◈ Hands too high or low
◈ Balance issues with horse or rider
◈ Legs too far forward
◈ Stirrups too long
◈ Poor selection of equipment

TIP 20 **The Turn**

Once the straight line approach, the rate for balance, and shortening of stride are achieved, the turn almost takes care of itself! Remind yourself that rating with two hands, especially on a green or strong horse, helps get the horse in the right position and ensures the horse's commitment to the turn. As the rate is achieved, the rider can shift her weight into the outside stirrup for support and stability. The inside seat bone is weighted and the rider's inside leg is light in the stirrup and slightly against the horse's inside rib. The center of the rider's chest turns at the same time as the horse's center chest begins to change directions into the turn. The rider's center chest should be pointing toward the horse's inside ear as the right shoulder and pelvis pivots into the turn. Once the all-important rate is achieved, the rider should practice riding one more stride into the turn before dropping the supporting outside rein and going to the horn. At this same time, the rider rides to the finish point of the turn and looks up to locate and establish the next pocket point and the line of approach into the next turn. Gather reins a stride or two off each barrel to ride once again with two hands into the next approach, rate, and turn sequence.

I feel the approach and the rate determine the success of the turn of each individual barrel.

TIP 21 **Common Errors in the Turn**

◈ Poor selection of pocket point
◈ Dropping leads
◈ Overuse of the inside or outside rein
◈ Lack of education on how to use the outside rein
◈ Loss of forward impulsion
◈ Hands too high or too low
◈ Balance issues with horse or rider
◈ Failure to finish the turn when horse does not answer rider's outside rein or leg
◈ Stirrups too long
◈ Ineffective equipment

TIP 22 Evaluating Performance for Consistent Competition

After each run the competitor and trusted performance coach should spend time evaluating the performance and identifying strengths and weaknesses that occurred during the competition. Once this identification has been made, a plan should be implemented for any retraining or correction necessary in order to prepare for the next competition. This is sometimes difficult while on the road, and a safe facility should be located. This concept is similar to the NASCAR race circuit. Between races the crew and driver identify areas of strengths and weaknesses that compliment or detract from peak performance. Usually before they leave a race they use the track to make necessary changes to the car to ready it for the next race. Changes are immediately implemented to complement good performance or modify and correct poor performance. I live by the rule, "Unless I win, I can't stay on the road." I need to be prepared to make each and every run count.

TIP 23 **Tips for Selecting a Horse Trailer for the Serious Hauler**

Hauling can be exhausting and stressful for both you and your horse. Investing in features that help keep your horse rested, sound, and safe are important. Most western horses are comfortable in trailers that are seven feet tall and eight feet wide with forty- to forty-two-inch slant stalls. Lined and insulated trailers with drop down doors on the front and back provide better ventilation and temperature control. If you do not have an air ride system, add Pro-cushion between the stall floors and the mats to reduce the bounce and shock. Hauling with shavings invites horses to urinate, while adding moisture and additional shock absorption. To tie or not to tie a horse's head in the trailer is always a decision. For safety purposes it may be the best option to "tie." Tying a horse prevents the horse from biting other horses, getting his head down under or over the divider, and it also helps stabilize the horse in stop-and-go traffic.

If hauling a single horse, avoid loading next to a solid wall or another place where you or the horse could be injured if he reacts badly to being loaded.

Consider buying a trailer with a ramp, as the newer trailers sit high off the ground. Ramps provide extra protection from rear-end accidents and they are safer for unloading horses on a variety of surfaces. Invest in good tires, a minimum of ten-ply to fourteen-ply if you have a living quarters, and always carry two spare tires. Check the air pressure on every trip and invest in the new pressure alert valve stems.

Hauling boots are good insurance in case a horse fights the trailer or bumps herself in traffic. Standing bandages also provide protection and support.

TIP 24 Never Lose Your Hat!

A lack of professional presence, fines, and inconvenience result when a rider loses her hat during a contest. First, make sure you are buying a hat that fits properly and complements your face. A stampede string can easily be added to any hat to help it stay in place. A squirt of hair spray on the sweatband also helps keep the hat in place. Personally, tucking the top of my ears into my hat always did the trick for me!

EIGHT

PROBLEM-SPECIFIC CORRECTIONS FOR BETTER BARREL RACING

If you want the best your horse has to offer, give your horse your best.

Taking Care of Business

Every time we turn on the news or listen to the radio we are reminded that our nation is facing some of the most serious challenges in its history. President Barack Obama said in one of his campaign speeches that "the strength of America is not shown in good times but character brought forth in times of tribulation." Rene Rapin wrote, "Our strength often increases in proportion to the obstacles which are imposed upon it," and a Chinese proverb reminds us that "the diamond cannot be polished without friction, nor the man perfected without trials."

There is very little difference between life and competition. A competitor in any discipline needs to be strong-minded and focused on the task at hand. A competitor needs to be goal-oriented in order to make decisions that keep her on the path to success. A true competitor knows when to press forward with purpose and when to withdraw and regroup with patience. What are you doing in these difficult times to strengthen yourself from within and guard against letting the real difficulties you may face rob you of your dream? It may be time to practice the patience part of success. It may be time to withdraw, and regroup. I am using these challenging times to reevaluate what is important in my life, taking time to focus on making those areas stronger and healthier. Again I say, I am optimistic that the challenges we each face today have the potential to leave us stronger, more self-confident, and more passionate toward the things in life that *really* matter.

Take the sport of barrel racing, for example. It is obviously a passion in our lives that not only comes with a horse and all its responsibilities, but it is also a lifestyle. A lifestyle built on hard work and honest sweat—decisions based on conservative values. No need to pay the high cost of a gym membership when calories can be burned cleaning stalls and lifting hay bales and sacks of feed!

Isn't it time to make the most of your competition dollars? It may be time to save some entry fee money and go to that clinic or seminar you've been putting off because there was another barrel race to go to, even if you haven't been placing or your horse has not been clocking. Take the time to watch an educational DVD or read that "how-to" book that has the potential of outlining the necessary steps to your success. Ask yourself, "Is it time to reassess my goals, focus on priorities, and take care of business?"

TIP 1 Problem-Specific Correction

Some problems need to be corrected at speed in the practice pen. Simulate a fast run to correct the problems that seem to only occur under the stress of competition. A competition bridle or training snaffle can be used for this correction. Choose the one that's most advantageous and gives the most control for correcting the particular problem.

TIP 2 Training and Remedial Work in the Round Pen

Remember that the resources of using a round pen are many. For a young horse, it is a safe environment to begin the training process, from the groundwork to the early rides. It is also a great area to introduce new equipment, work on smooth and balanced gait transitions, and reinforce a rider's body position. The round pen is a good "time-out" for volatile horses, and an area to work on suppleness and even begin the introduction and focus on cattle. The sizes of the round pen and construction vary according to environment and discipline. The larger the diameter, the more room you have to be creative in the instruction. However, when starting horses, a smaller diameter helps keep closer contact and allows less evasion. Be creative and design the environment for your job at hand.

The resources of the round pen are far beyond just training the young horse. Older horses or competition horses that need to return to some basic training for review or correction can go into the pen to work out issues. The round pen is a good place to

introduce bit or equipment changes without the influence of the rider on his back. For barrel racing, if the round pen is large enough, one or two barrels can be set up and exercises incorporated off the rim of the pen. Again, be creative. Often we are only limited by our imagination, and the round pen is a valuable resource throughout the life of any performance horse.

TIP 3 **Double Down**

The double down exercise has several names, depending on the trainer you are talking to. The bottom line is that we all use some form of this exercise to defuse problems and remind the horse who is driving! The double down is a multi-use positive correction that is used when a horse fails to respond to the request to move forward in the alleyway, fails to respond or balks in backing, tries to rear, or resists the rider's command. The maneuver can also be utilized as a time-out to reestablish the horse's attention on the rider.

At the point when the horse fails to respond to the rider's request to move forward or resists the rider's commands, pull the horse's head firmly toward your knee. Use both legs at the front cinch to request the horse to move forward at a jog in a small circle. Sit your trot.

Maintain constant pressure on the rein and forward motion of the horse's feet. Five to six rotations are appropriate in order to reestablish the horse's attention and engage movement throughout the horse's body.

Once forward motion is obtained, use the inside leg to bump the horse in the flank area to disengage the hindquarters. If the front legs are not moving forward, kick with both legs at the front cinch to engage forward. This prevents the horse from pivoting on his front-end. This is not a pretty exercise—it is a discipline.

After five or six circles check to see if the horse's inside ear has turned to focus on the rider. At this point he is saying, "Oh, there is a rider on my back, and what was it you were asking me to do?" Allow the horse another opportunity to respond to the rider's initial request.

If the horse refuses, return to the double-down correction in either direction.

As soon as the horse attempts to respond, praise, reward, but *do not stop* the forward motion, and confidently return to work.

Remember the importance of consistent reward and discipline. Don't "pick" at the horse to get the point across. The horse needs to understand that his refusal to respond to the rider's request is not acceptable. Good luck!

TIP 4 Be Aware of Your Saddle Fit

The majority of saddle trees are constructed of dried and aged hardwood and covered with rawhide for support and stability. The leather saddle parts are then screwed or stapled in place and the felt or sheepskin that covers the under bar is glued in place. A

broken or cracked bar can cause instability and soreness, as will a protruding screw or staple. The goal is to have the bars of the saddle mirror the shape of the horse's back with no sharp objects hiding within the camouflage of the sheepskin. Run your hand across the sheepskin to check for sharp or protruding objects that may have worked loose. Remain aware that the wooden tree can crack or break and should be replaced immediately if it does. Equipment fatigue is also an issue to be aware of. Each saddling is an opportunity to check over your equipment. It may be a good rule of thumb to replace the latigo and billet on an annual basis, depending on how often you ride throughout the year.

TIP 5   Gate Issues

Almost every barrel racing horse experiences some anxiety about entering the gate prior to making a competition run. This is all part of the horse's process of learning how to deal with the pressure and adrenaline of competition. The more confidence the horse has in the rider, the easier it is to minimize and overcome gate issues. We gain that confidence through building a solid foundation and maintaining our horse's attention and respect. By developing the ability to control the different zones, or parts, of our horse's body, we can more easily align and control the direction we send our horse.

To gain our horse's confidence it is very important that we do not change the rules. When it is time to enter the gate, sit with a deep, quiet seat until your horse enters the arena. When making your run, only ask for as much from your horse as you have asked for at home. Use the same cues and techniques that you have practiced with your horse. By being consistent your horse learns to trust you and gains confidence in his own abilities.

TIP 6 Common Causes of Alley or Gate Problems

It is not uncommon for barrel horses to develop gate or alleyway issues. Though the issues are correctable in most instances, the best course of action is not to let them develop in the first place. Potential causes of alley or gate difficulties are:

◈ A nervous horse, feeding off of a nervous rider

◈ Lack of confidence of the horse and/or the rider

◈ Failure to properly prepare for competition

◈ Ulcers

◈ Improperly adjusted or ill-fitting equipment, including the bit, pad, or saddle

◈ Ineffective schooling and correction

Fear:

◈ of being pushed too fast

◈ of hitting a barrel

◈ of uncertain ground and/or falling

◈ of being whipped, jerked on, or unjustified kicking and spurring

◈ of increasing discomfort from an already painful and sore body part

◈ of the unknown

◈ of internal bleeding causing restriction of air source

TIP 7 Making the Decision to Circle Before a Barrel Run

Circling a horse prior to a run can be beneficial if it is done with a purpose. Use this circle to ensure your horse is on the proper lead to turn the first barrel, soften your horse to your hands and legs, balance him from head to tail, and line him up for a smooth start. Be sure to plan the size of your circle and where you want to start from to go to your first barrel. Make your circle big enough to keep your horse moving forward with

impulsion and to enable you to make any corrections in a forward motion. Correcting your horse and getting him responsive in your circle is quickly accomplished by practicing these skills at home. Once your horse knows his proper body position and is familiar with your cues, your adjustments and transition to eliminating the circle prior to the barrel run can be made efficiently and effectively. It takes mental and physical preparation to achieve a fast and smooth first barrel turn. A major ingredient of an efficient first barrel is an effective pre-race warm-up routine. The first barrel is an integral part of a winning run as it sets the pace and rhythm for the entire race.

TIP 8 Exercises to Smooth Out Rough Barrel Turns

Several circumstances can create a rough turn. Common problems like approaching in the incorrect lead, beginning the turn too early and causing the horse's shoulder or rib to drop towards the barrel, bunny-hopping with both hind legs, or dropping leads in the turn, all result in a horse's loss of balance and forward momentum. Loss of momentum results in disappointing performance.

In practice, try working a horse who is making rough turns a stride deeper on the backside of the turn (between barrel and fence). Focus on sitting deep, cue for collection by riding two-handed, and use the support of the outside rein. Re-circle the barrel and increase the size of the correcting circle to approximately twenty feet on all sides of the barrel. Apply leg pressure to help move the horse forward and collected into the larger circle. This larger circle relaxes and helps the horse rebalance. Slight leg pressure at the outside and back cinch area supports the correct lead, while the use of the inside leg softens the rib and enhances fluid turns. Make sure to maintain connection of the reins to help stabilize the horse's head and shoulders. Once the horse relaxes, complete perhaps one to three circles, then prepare to tighten up the circle and ride into your barrel turn. Leave extra room on the back side of the barrel and complete the turn, riding on to the next barrel.

Placing the outside hand on the horse's hip can help relax and encourage the horse to keep driving forward.

TIP 9 Addressing the Uncontrollable Horse

Frustration for the horse and rider is the result of trying to take a horse to the barrel pattern without a foundation. It remains your responsibility to know when to back off and return to fundamental training and when to seek knowledgeable advice if you feel either you or the horse is becoming frustrated. Do not run a horse that has training issues that haven't been addressed. They just get worse. The unfortunate reality is that untrained horses can be patterned to run barrels without being physically or mentally prepared. These horses, though patterned, do not have the education or skills to hold it together as speed is increased. It is only a short time until the horse outruns his ability or training level. This becomes a dangerous and frustrating situation and the horse is often sold, along with the problem, and passed from one rider to another.

Although the decision is not easy, in this situation it is time to take a few steps back and address the holes in the horse's foundation. Teach the horse to accept the application of pressure without fear or resentment. This process begins in the halter. Most horses that resist pressure in the bridle also resist at this level. The trick to getting the horse to soften to pressure is learning to have perfect timing, using the release of pressure to soften, reward, and encourage the horse as he learns to yield to pressure. This process is not easily explained in a few paragraphs. I would suggest exploring any of the works of Ray Hunt, Tom Dorrance, or Buck Brannaman to understand the thought behind this process of releasing pressure. *The Western Horseman* has some excellent colt-starting and problem-solving books in their library.

Physical issues should also be considered for horses that all of the sudden appear to be uncontrollable. For example, dental issues can create resistance, just as sore backs, sore feet, or sore hocks can.

TIP 10   Calming the Volatile Horse

Some barrel horses are volatile and explosive. It is my experience that the more escape routes they are given, the more they begin to feed on their own volatility. Educate your horse to accept rein contact. When you feel your horse begin to lose focus in training or warm-up, give him an exercise to do a maneuver that involves some head to tail bend. A lateral step or side pass is usually enough to return the horse's attention to the rider and reduce his anxiety.

A training snaffle bit used in combination with a cowboy German martingale is a good bridle and aid choice to help keep a horse in between a rider's hands, which eliminates escape routes. The cowboy German martingale also helps collect the horse from head to tail and may prove to be effective equipment in pre-game warm-up as well as during training sessions.

Feeding the volatile horse a low-energy diet and increasing his fat content has also proven to be effective in calming the attitude.

TIP 11 How to Liven Up a Lazy Horse

Make sure your horse is focused on you. He needs to be interested enough to answer your over/under when you pick it up. If the horse is dull to the request there are a variety of ways to get him tuned into the rider. Gallop your horse in a large sixty-foot circle, ask first with a smooch or kiss, apply leg pressure, and if there is not a significant burst of speed, pick up the over/under and use it—like you mean it—once.

I would also check out your feed program. Often a lazy or laid-back horse could benefit from a higher energy feed; research the 14-percent protein options. This may be the time to check your horse's blood count for indications of anemia and for organ functions that could affect performance.

Leather noseband tie downs often give the horse a little resistance to run into the bit or bridle. Consider using the leather noseband if needed for accurate performance. Regardless of what some riders say, the properly adjusted tie down offers a balance point to horses in the timed-event classes.

The bottom line is that some horses, though very athletic and capable, just don't like the event well enough or have the heart to exert the consistent effort necessary to run out each and every race. These horses usually won't make a professional caliber or consistent 1D horse, but are patterned and make great horses for less-aggressive riders that don't need to ask them for their lives each and every run.

TIP 12 Creating Incentives for a Lazy Barrel Horse

There are several possibilities to consider for sparking a horse's interest to produce extra effort in competition. However, the reality is that some horses like the sport and clock in spite of their credentials. Others just don't have the natural incentive, regardless of their breeding or athletic ability, to put forth a winning effort. First off and most

obvious: is the horse sound? Next, check your equipment. Make sure your saddle and pad fit and are not binding the horse's shoulders or inhibiting his stride. When your horse runs comfortably without aches and pains it makes a big difference in his effort and confidence.

Next evaluate the feed. If it appears that he feels like running, try increasing his calories. I have used Omolene 200 and Platform Performance for a little extra zip on horses that feel flat or too laid back. Also use joint products with Omega fats. I recommend the Equine Essentials by Noni. Eleven-time world champion Charmayne James also uses this product. Noni helps maximize oxygen intake and utilization, which can be very important at higher altitudes.

In the area of conditioning, make sure your horse feels like giving you the 110 percent it takes to run top times. Galloping out and long trotting help build lung capacity and stride. Also incorporate monthly one hundred to two hundred and fifty yard sprints into your conditioning program. Make sure the horse understands that when you ask him with a smooch or chase him with an over/under that he understands to give you *all* he has, and feels like doing it.

- Work on *efficient* performance. Remember to ride straight and deep, expecting collection and balanced turns. Work on your ability to extend and collect your horse at a variety of speeds without a lot of begging or effort.
- When you look at shoeing, make sure your horse's feet are balanced and that his shoes offer the necessary foundation and support.
- Returning to reality, some horses are very capable. However, call it smarts or call it heart, they protect themselves by not giving that extra effort into and out of a barrel. If you take the fraction of a second, say one-tenth going into a turn, another one-tenth leaving, multiply that by three barrels, and you have a disadvantage of one-half of a second before you ever hear your time.
- A critical tip: listen to your performance coach and work together to maximize your performance, pre-game warm-up, mental game, soundness, nutrition, and conditioning.
- Thousands of horses are started on the barrels each year. For a multitude of reasons, only a very small number fall into the "great" category. Education, evaluation, and management help us maximize our opportunities for success.

TIP 13 Creating a Balanced Approach

Going to the horn too early reinforces the horse's tendency to drop or move into the barrel. Dropping the outside rein before the horse is in balanced position for his rate and turn is one of the major causes of poor performance among riders. Practice riding two-handed, one hand on each side of the reins, to help ride and balance the horse on the established line of approach toward the barrel. Timing is critical. Try riding into the barrel two-handed and rate two-handed before dropping the outside rein and going to the horn on the back side of your barrel, just before the horse finishes the turn and strides out to the next barrel. Holding onto the horn a stride or two away from the barrel also helps the rider maintain a balanced body position and leads to a more efficient performance.

TIP 14 The Importance of Using the Outside Rein

The use of the inside, direct rein indicates to the horse the direction the rider is asking him to travel. The outside, indirect rein is the other half of the control equation and aids in the alignment of the horse's outside rib and shoulder. Wow! Sounds like the secret many of us have never thought about using. In barrel racing, we learn how to ride the inside, turning rein, but little is said about the importance of the outside rein.

The outside rein helps balance and stabilize the horse in the approach. The outside rein helps keep the outside shoulder under the horse in the rate and turn. The outside rein helps shorten and control the inside hock, the leg our horses use to balance themselves as they move into and around the turn. The outside rein is also the rein used to control speed. The thoughtful application of both reins are required to create a balanced head carriage and level and balanced shoulders, and it helps control the speed and collection of the barrel horse. It takes equal and proper use of both reins to balance and stabilize the horse. A good rider *never* uses the reins for rider balance.

TIP 15 The Dangers of Incorporating Too Much Bend in the Barrel Turn

Remember that the outside rein offers the rider the opportunity to set and balance the horse's head and neck. The outside rein also captures the energy generated by the rider's seat and legs and helps create forward movement. Too much nose in a turn can disengage the horse's outside shoulder and allow the hip to step out, creating lateral movement and slower turns. Too much inside rein or leg may also cause a horse to drop a lead behind and sling his hindquarters away from the turn.

Any lateral movement dramatically and negatively affects fast times as the horse loses his forward momentum. If you feel this stall as you leave your barrel use both legs together, squeezing from hips to calf, to create the energy needed to move the front end of the horse forward. The over/under on the backside of the barrel can be used to reinforce or increase impulsion.

TIP 16 Corrections for Horses That Resist the Bit During a Competition Run

If your horse only flips his nose and resists the bit in competition it may be difficult to institute a correction. However, with attention on riding you may find this is an issue during every ride inside or out of the arena, especially as speed and pressure is increased. Once noticed, take steps to redirect the behavior. Focus should be placed on the rider's seat, legs, and reins. Make sure the horse moves forward on request, add a German martingale to help remove the horse's escape routes, cue for a leg yield, and double down or visit the round pen for upward, downward, and lateral transition exercises. These are all creative ways to interrupt the horse's poor behavioral choices. The round pen also helps correct evasion of the bit pressure. If you have not already done so, this is the time to contact your veterinarian to rule out any physical or dental issues that may be causing the problem.

If this problem truly only occurs in competition, I suggest it is a rider's balance problem. Make sure not to get left behind leaving the barrel, which results in the rider pulling back on the reins as an attempt to regain balance. Check stirrup length to make sure the stirrups are not too long, which would contribute to poor balance. Once the rider can maintain control and balance throughout the barrel pattern, I would suggest adding a leather noseband tie down to help balance the horse's head and remind him not to flip him nose.

TIP 17 Building More Snap in Your Turn

In the sport of barrel racing, our judge is the electric timer or stopwatch. It is not a subjective or judged event. Efficiency is the key to fast times and consistent performance. There may come a time when the runs you are producing are smooth and the horse is running well in-between barrels, but your times are still off the pace. If this happens, try working for additional snap in your turn. This requires livening up the horse's feet, inviting quickness and stride without losing rhythm. Circle your horse on the barrel turn, prepare for the exercise by placing reins in the inside turning hand, and move the over/under to the outside of the turn. Kiss or smooch and ask your horse by applying leg to pick up his feet and move lighter and faster through the turn. Tap or over/under on the outside hip to influence more energy. This also helps prepare a horse to liven his feet in preparation for runs in deep or heavy ground.

Like all exercises, move the horse off the barrel pattern to experiment with the technique. On a big circle, approximately fifty feet in diameter, gather the reins with the inside hand, and prepare the over/under or bat in the outside hand. Kiss, squeeze with legs, use the over/under or bat *one* time to influence faster forward. Let the horse move out several strides, relax, and regain control. Always test your results. Kiss again, apply leg, and if the horse produces the required response, *do not* use the over/under or whip. Relax and pet your horse for his response. Effective training gives a new definition to the word "forward." When offered, the horse needs to respond to the verbal command for forward.

TIP 18 Evaluating Behavioral Issues During Competition

Erratic behavior in competition is not only unacceptable—it is dangerous. Serious evaluation should be considered and questions answered in order to solve potential problems. Consider the following checklist:

◈ Is the horse medically sound?

◈ Sometimes horses that display this behavior can be having breathing difficulties. It is stated in the literature that 80 percent of the speed horses "bleed." Horses that display panicked responses in the arena could be having, or could have had in the past, some degree of pulmonary hemorrhage. Check with your veterinarian about the possibility.

◈ If there appears to be no soundness issues, is it a training deficit?

◈ Your horse should be educated so that he is easily adjusted, regardless of the speed he is traveling, by utilizing your aids and sequencing your cues. The horse needs to be educated to respond to the rider's requests. It is said that your horse needs to respond to a whisper of an aid, not a shout.

◈ Do you have the correct equipment on your horse?

◈ Equipment needs to be effective and should be selected with the individual horse's strengths and weaknesses in mind. Check to see if the equipment is adjusted correctly. Check to see that the equipment is not malfunctioning or pinching. A horse should not pull through your bridle and should carry the control with confidence and respect.

◈ Could these behavioral problems be induced by diet?

◈ Try cutting out grain and supplements and substituting them with a good quality, low-protein grass hay. The addition of fat in a horse's diet can also have a calming

effect. Tryptophan, the indigent in turkey that makes us lazy on a Thanksgiving afternoon, is available for horses in Quietex by Farnam, and Vita Calm by Animed. Equilite makes a product, Relax Blend, containing natural herbs. I have also seen calming results by feeding vitamin B1. It may be beneficial to research the options of incorporating neutraceuticals into your feed program. It may take some experimentation to see which resource works the best on your horse. I have had excellent results with these products. As always, consultation with your veterinarian is advised.

NINE

BUILDING CONFIDENCE AND GAINING THE WINNING EDGE

Experience is the best teacher, but only if we become the best student.

My Heroes Have Always Been Cowgirls—Empowering Your Dreams

Dale Evans, the most famous of silver-screen cowgirls, said, "Cowgirl is an attitude, a pioneer spirit, a special American brand of courage.

"The cowgirl faces life head on, lives by her own lights, and makes no excuses. Cowgirls take stands, they speak up, and they defend the things they hold dear."

Reid Slaughter, publisher and executive editor of *Cowboys and Indians Magazine*, describes cowgirls as women of character who in the early days were outnumbered by their male counterparts, almost seven to one, and yet managed to survive and thrive in their personal frontiers. Today's cowgirl might wield a cell phone and drive a sport utility vehicle, but she carries in her heart that same spirit of adventure. Like her sisters before her, she rides into each day with a passion for life and an underlying strength that comes from healthy self-reliance.

Just as America and the West continue to change and develop, so does the cowgirl. Today she lives in the city as well as the country. She pilots a plane as well as rides a horse. She runs a bank as well as manages a ranch. She has that cowgirl spirit inherited from generations of remarkable women who went before her, and she is using it to pioneer new worlds from the Supreme Court to new technologies.

My heroes have always been cowgirls. From my earliest recollection of watching Dale Evans and Buttermilk prevail against all odds I have had a passion to pursue my cowgirl dreams.

My parents insisted that every young aspiring "cowgirl" needed an education to fall back on in case the initial plan failed. However, my perseverance paid off. Donning my cowgirl hat, I pursued my passion by blending my academic degree and equestrian knowledge to carve a notch in the belt of the equine industry.

Truly, women and horses have a special bond. Very few of us have not dreamt of owning and caring for our own horse. The vision creates a sense of empowerment and freedom. Though a passing phase for some, horses have been partners throughout my life and are a huge part of my career.

I remind myself on a daily basis how truly blessed we are to have the chance to live in a country that offers us the opportunity to pursue our dreams and goals. Though life is not always green pastures and smooth rides, each challenge and celebration we face offers us the opportunity to strengthen our personal core and character.

Life is a learning opportunity and for those of us who choose to face life head on, live by our own light, and see the glass half full instead of half empty, it truly is a great life! May I serve as a reminder to those of you who share a passion and a purpose to stay strongly focused on your goals, to find ways to empower your dreams. Often our success is only limited by our imagination and our determination.

I invite anyone who has the patience to pursue excellence solely for the challenge, not the expectation of reward, to relish in the daily challenges that serve as a reminder that a well-lived life is nothing more than a series of accomplished days.

Honor your passion. Find a reward in each day. Learn to laugh out loud. Don't take yourself too seriously, and dance, even if you can't hear the music.

Saddle Your Own Horse

One of the lessons of the Cowgirl Hall of Fame in Fort Worth, Texas, is that the only way to do things with purpose and to our personal satisfaction is to do it yourself! Saddling your own horse makes a bigger statement than the obvious. It gives you an opportunity to get a sense of your horse's attitude before you climb on. It gives you an opportunity to check the condition of your equipment, and the brushing and grooming process that takes place before the saddle goes on,

gives you a chance to scope out the physical condition of your horse. Teach your horse to stand patiently during grooming and saddling.

"Always saddle your own horse"
—Connie Reeves, CHF

TIP 2

Everyone Loves a Winner

Winning is easy; it is the losing that takes practice. Just remember that neither outcome is permanent. As a competitor, I expect to win, and obviously I am disappointed when I don't. I treat that condition as a personal issue and try not to impose my disappointment on others. Evaluate your attitude and your performance and establish how to turn the next run into a winning experience.

TIP 3 | Success Is Contagious—So Is Failure

Positive attitudes are contagious. Learn to select your competitive friends and mentors wisely.

Your choice of friends and travel companions are as important to your success as your winning run. Read positive literature, listen to positive music, learn to think positive thoughts, and eliminate negative statements from your vocabulary. Positive attitudes create winning environments. Surrounding yourself with negative influences is as destructive to successful competition as a knocked-over barrel.

TIP 4 Filtering Information

We live in a world where information is readily available. There are many instructional DVDs and books. There are a variety of clinics and camps available throughout the world. RFD Television is an additional venue to market ideas and information. Whether buying information, equipment, or philosophy, use your good common sense in selecting the resource that best supports and builds on your personal interest and venue. The outcome of

any choice must be a win-win for the related parties. The seller wants your money; you want the product or information. Practice common sense in all your decisions. If you continue to have questions, ask a trusted professional for his input.

TIP 5 Creating a Winning Combination

My entire program and competitive philosophy is based on traditional horsemanship and the importance of creating a strong foundation and a responsive horse. If your new horse is broke and has a good foundation, then it is a matter of the horse learning a little of the rider's ways and the rider adapting a little to the horse's ways. Be patient. Odds are it will take a year for the horse and rider to gain confidence in each other.

If the new horse demonstrates a lack of control or is rude in his manners, I say, regardless of his age, that his fundamentals are weak. Start the process of education and discipline. I don't think it is an unreasonable request to be the driver when I am on a hard-running horse in a barrel race. I want the horse listening to me rather than just responding to the pattern.

Barrel racing is a sport, and not a style of riding. My teaching philosophy is the creation of a balanced, effective rider and a relaxed, responsive horse. The bit is a tool to communicate with the horse in training and at a high rate of speed in competition. I believe in the use of training, tuning, direct control, and equipment with the addition of an appropriate martingale to keep the horses soft and supple. In addition, I select two bits in the competitive category that complement each other, in order to have an option depending on the circumstances of each competition. These three bits create what I refer to as a "biting triangle" appropriate for the training and improvement of the individual horse I am working with.

I want to know that the horse is safe for me to ride, enters the arena without resistance, and is responsive in the run. I encourage riders young or old, experienced or novice, to purchase horses that build confidence and produce safe rides.

TIP 6
Don't Lose the Lesson

We are all a work in progress at one level or another. Each challenge we survive only prepares us and makes us stronger for the next. Remember, when failure does enter the picture, you may lose the race or contest, but just don't lose the lesson.

TIP 7 **Dressing for Success**

How you look and feel about yourself is a big part of building competitive confidence. Enter the arena in warm-up and competition with your chin up and your eyes forward. Put some energy and presence in your horse's gait. Dress appropriately for the discipline with clean, well-prepared clothing. Your horse should be clean and well-groomed and your equipment should show the same care and attention.

Learn to emulate success and "act as if" you have already achieved it. Study other successful riders to learn their secrets to success. Most importantly, never be intimidated to ask for advice.

TIP 8 Believe in Yourself!

Possibilities emerge for those who are prepared, for those who are ready. World All-Around Cowboy Champion Larry Mahan once made the statement, "Luck is where preparation meets opportunity." Believe in yourself and stay true to your dreams and goals. This is where purpose, patience, and passion enter into the equation for success. The road to success takes a map. Once you identify where you want to end up you can begin to chart your course.

For an example, if you want to travel from California to New York, you would look for the most direct route. Heading toward Canada or Hawaii obviously takes you away from the direct path. If you end up there, that demonstrates that the priority to arrive as soon as possible was not important and the beaches of Hawaii looked inviting. Don't be disappointed; the decision to deviate from your path was your choice.

The most important part of identifying the journey is to learn to make choices that contribute to reaching the destination. It is obviously easier for younger riders to establish a path because their support system is in place. I remind students that their parents are their biggest champions. Though some of us are not as privileged as others, or may be beginning our journey later in life, consider the opportunities. Often we are only limited by our imaginations, and it really is true: Where there is a will there is a way. But, first and most important, find your passion, establish your course, make decisions that keep you on track, and believe in yourself!

TIP 9 Leave the Arena with a Smile, and Be Grateful for the Experience

Let's face it: not all of our runs are going to be perfect. Sometimes our mistakes are major ones. We all get embarrassed from time to time, but jerking, spurring, or whipping our horses as we leave the arena teaches the horse nothing, and it truly makes us look bad. You have two choices when a mistake happens during a run. You can use your run and make a quick correction right there where the mistake happened, or at the following barrel if the situation allows. If you choose to do this, don't lose your temper, don't waste everyone's time, and don't tear up the ground for the next rider. Make your correction and then go on with the rest of your run. An alternate choice is that after you run, head back to the practice pen, set up the same situation, and make your corrections at that time. Let your horse make the same mistake before you make your correction. Don't expect him to remember what he did during the run. Regardless of what choice you make, leave the arena with your rein hand down, head held high, and a smile on your face.

TIP 10 Count Your Blessings

Love what you are doing, be grateful for your opportunities, and count your blessings for having the good fortune to live in an environment that allows you the freedom and the economic resources to pursue your dreams and goals!

Does it mean that you are going to love every minute of your riding experience or win every race you enter? No, probably not. Riding in inclement weather conditions is not always fun, nor is caring for your horses when you would rather be doing something else. However, it does mean that you are living your dream of being a horse owner and reminds you to appreciate your opportunity.

TIP 11 Ride as Many Good Horses as You Can

We always talk about a "good" horse, but until you have a chance to ride one, that feeling is difficult to define or even imagine. It is hard to identify the results you are training for if you have never felt them. I believe that top barrel racers that have had one good horse in their career usually can duplicate the feel on other horses. Charmayne James won ten world championships on her great horse, Scamper, and her eleventh world championship on Cruiser. Winning runs are forward, efficient, and effortless. It truly is racing the stopwatch, and until you feel that pace, it is hard to train. Though cultivating speed is critical, it is the timing and rhythm that is most important.

Early in my career, former world champion Lynn McKenzie invited me to ride her great horse Magnolia Missile. Wow! Any place you sent him he went effortlessly, without resistance or hesitation. Ah ha! So *this* is what a winning horse feels like!

Not everyone can just take a ride on a horse the caliber of Missile, or have a friend that would make that contribution to your career like Lynn did for me. But, on the other hand, what does it hurt to ask? Perhaps you are taking lessons from somebody who has experienced successful competition. If they have faith in your ability, ask. All they can do say is no, and who knows, maybe they will say yes.

TIP 12 Ride as Many Different Horses as You Can

Whenever you get the chance, ride different horses. However, caution needs to be taken to avoid unsafe horses that could possibly be dangerous. I make a point not to ride horses that rear, and obviously I do not choose to climb on a horse that bucks!

Riding a variety of horses gives a rider the opportunity to expand his timing and rhythm and to learn to adapt to a variety of animals, each with its own style and personality. Talented horses come in all shapes, sizes, conformations, and breeds. Ultimately, the more horses you ride the quicker you learn to adapt and understand, as a rider, what you need to do to create an enjoyable experience for both you and the horse.

If you have the opportunity, choose to ride with riders who are better than you and try to ride horses that are better trained than yours. This offers a great learning opportunity. A good rule of thumb, though, is to not try to climb on and immediately put the horse through his paces, no matter how trained the horse is. As a young aspiring cowgirl, I had the chance to ride my first real cow horse. Thrilled with the opportunity, I began to sit tall, puff my chest, and put the horse through its paces. I had often watched the owner with awe and envy as they worked the very horse I was riding. The old cowboy watched with a grin. "Gal," he said, "the quickest way to make a fool of you and your horse is to try to show all you know before you know what it is you do know. Just ride out and let the horse teach you a thing or two."

Today, I find a few trotting and loping circles tells me more about my ride than trying to put the horse through his paces too quickly. Each horse offers us an opportunity to learn a lesson, some good, others not so good, each contributing in its own way to our goal of becoming better riders and horseman. Enjoy your lesson; enjoy the ride!

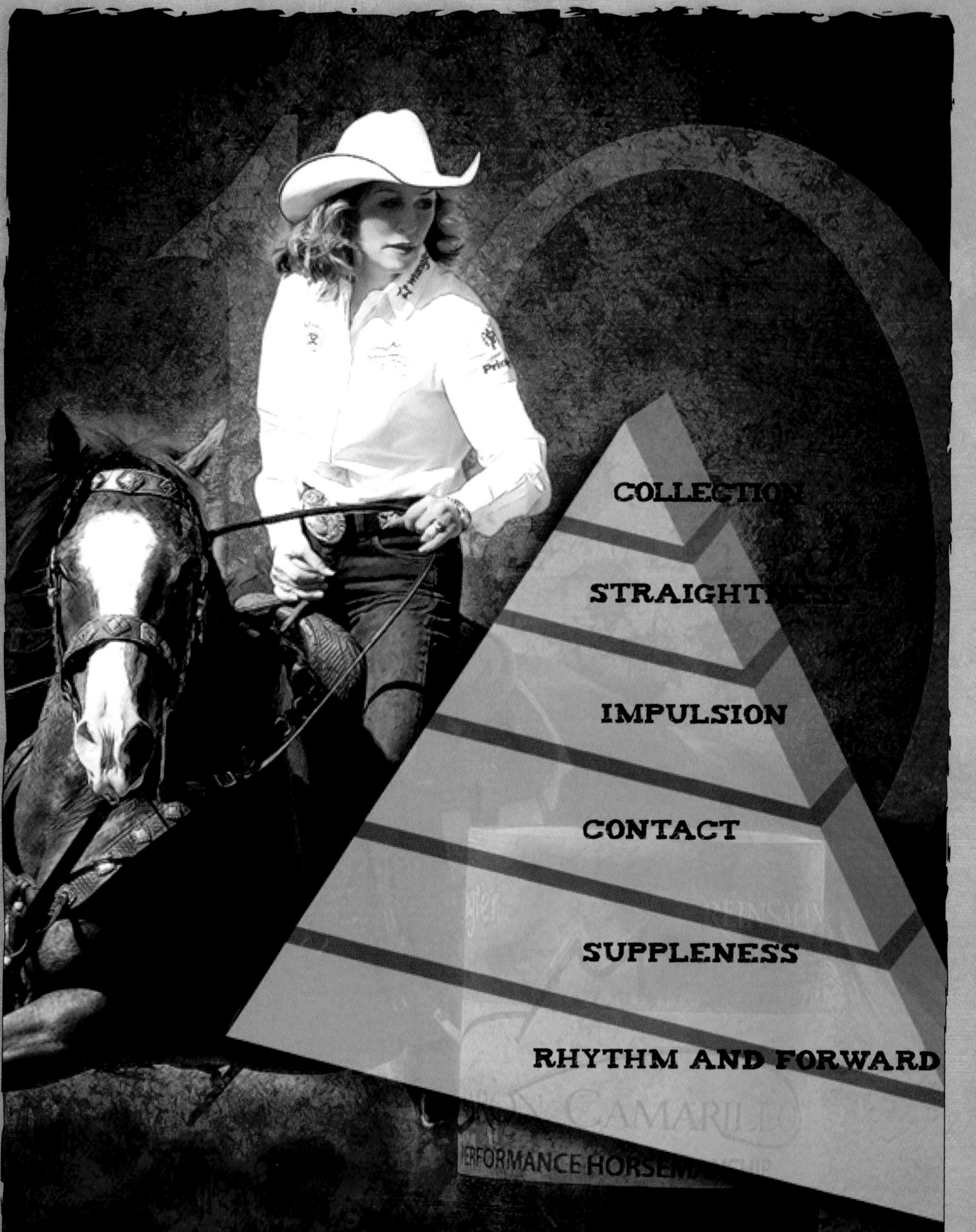

COLLECTION

STRAIGHTNESS

IMPULSION

CONTACT

SUPPLENESS

RHYTHM AND FORWARD

CAMARILLO

PERFORMANCE HORSEMANSHIP

TEN

THE TRAINING
PYRAMID

*Life is a persistent teacher. It will keep
repeating the lesson until we learn.*

Utilizing the Training
Pyramid for Better Barrel Racing

As a self-proclaimed student of horsemanship, my goal is to learn to communicate with horses to gain mutually beneficial results. Horses are not disposable commodities. We owe it to them to develop their full potential, and along the way we should evaluate and develop our own. We love our association with the horse and all that he represents. I hate to see them exploited or abused. I have come to understand that good horses have a better chance of having good lives, and God knows our good horses deserve the best lives.

World champion trainer Bob Avila said, "Since the horse does not have the ability to think correct body position for himself, the rider has to do it for him. This puts more responsibility on the rider to take the reins and make it happen."

My goal in utilizing the training pyramid for better barrel racing is to put focus on the skills our horses need to achieve self-carriage. If we pay attention, our student, the horse, becomes the teacher. The techniques used in the training pyramid also make each of us better riders.

Through building rhythm and forward, combining suppleness and collection for a strong top line, and achieving straightness and ultimately collection, you will be surprised and well rewarded, not only with increased communication and a more enjoyable ride, but you will be entertained and excited to see how these skills carry over to how a horse carries himself in play in the pasture without a rider on his back! Enjoy the journey and enjoy the ride!

TIP 1
Understanding the Training Pyramid

The six building blocks of the training pyramid are essential elements in creating and reinforcing the skills necessary to produce athletic and balanced performance in any and all equestrian disciplines. All serious riders should incorporate skill exercises into their routines to reinforce the following movements and maneuvers in their daily riding as well as in pre-event warm-ups.

TIP 2 Rhythm and Forward

Rhythm and forward are the regular and rhythmic footfalls of the horse's gaits. Rhythm is the foundation of everything we do, or plan to do. Rhythm incorporates the horse's ability to move freely forward. When the movement of the horse becomes erratic or rough, back off to the speed where rhythm returns to the stride. Like music, the horse's footfalls should keep up with the beats of the song.

TIP 3 Suppleness

A horse that is supple has the ability to bend and flex in the body "zones" laterally and longitudinally in a relaxed, fluid, and willing manner. This skill should be introduced and reinforced in the direct control bit of choice.

153

TIP 4 Contact

The horse needs to respect and accept the pressure applied to the bit by the rider's hands. This includes the horse's willingness to move forward into the bit without resistance or hesitation. This skill allows the rider to connect the horse from tail to head, haunches to forehand. The round pen is a great resource to introduce forward and connection to the green, unwilling, or intimated horse. Responsible and consistent communication between the horse and rider is the key to success. Be responsible and aware of responses, cues, and commands.

TIP 5 Impulsion

Impulsion is forward propulsion created from the power generated from the hind end forward. The movement enables forward, lateral, and reverse maneuvers, including stops and turnarounds.

TIP 6 Straightness

Straightness is the ability of the rider to align the horse's body on straight and curved lines for efficient, effective, and balanced movement. Straightness requires attention by the rider and the application of the rider's aids: seat, legs, and hands. Straightness also requires application of the skills provided by the prior levels of the training pyramid.

TIP 7 Collection

The ultimate reward of applying the skills provided by the training pyramid is to teach a horse to carry his body in an athletic manner with little reminder or support from the rider. This is called "self-carriage." Collection allows the rider to lengthen and shorten the horse's stride, control speed, and provides the ability to consistently place the horse's body in a balanced, athletic position for efficient movement. One warning: don't get confused with head set versus true collection. When truly collected, from head to tail, the horse can then engage his natural drive train—his rear end—for forward power. This is the philosophy of performance horsemanship for better barrel racing.

Additional Pearls of Information

The goal of the Sharon Camarillo Performance Horsemanship for Better Barrel Racing Clinic is to introduce concepts, teach and reinforce skills designed to produce precise and consistent Approach, Rate, and Turn, evaluate performance, and address problem-specific corrections for the satisfaction and well being of both the horse and rider.

SHARON CAMARILLO
would like to thank these friends and sponsors:
American Quarter Horse Association; Amarillo, Texas Professional Horseman

Beth Cross, Ariat International; Union City, California

Dick and Brooks Atwood, Atwood Hat Company; Frankston, Texas

Lucky King, Bandera of California; Murphys, California

Black Hawk College; Kewanee, Illinois

Jimmy and Kathy Court, Tony Court, Jennifer Wilson; Court's Saddlery, Bryan, Texas

Pete Melnicker, Double Diamond Halters; Gallatin Gateway, Montana

Heather Hoff, Deanna Finnie, Farnam Companies, Inc.; Phoenix, Arizona

Gary Gist, Jennifer Folsom, Wende Heinin, Gist Silversmiths; Placerville, California

Bill Priefert, David Fillebrown, Priefert; Mt. Pleasant, Texas

Denise Calef, Art Director, ProSportsPix; Penn Valley, California

Bob Brandon, Dale Martin, Reinsman Equestrian Products, Inc.; Cleveland, Tennessee

S. A. Walls, Walls Stirrups; Mena, Arkansas

Jeff Chadwick, Pam Baker, Wrangler; Greensboro, North Carolina

SHARON CAMARILLO
would like to thank the following photographers:
Ron Calef, Prosportspix • Cyndy Smith • Robin Hayes • Cindy Chaffin

SHARON CAMARILLO
would like to thank her Performance Team and other friends
used in the photographs:
Jin Berry • Bobbi Jo Bohlman • Cristina Borregales • Mark Brum

Katie Chaffin • Susie Gunter • Carly Hagey • David Hayes

Kallen Hayes • Jessica Hull • Donna Irvin

Lauren Pai • Cheryl Price • Jim Price • Diane Purcelli • Susan Van Rein